MANCS

VS.

SCOUSERS

2

MANCS START HERE

First published 2009
by Black & White Publishing Ltd
29 Ocean Drive, Edinburgh EH6 6JL

1 3 5 7 9 10 8 6 4 2   09 10 11 12 13

ISBN: 978 1 84502 277 8

A CIP catalogue record for this book is available from the British Library.

Typeset by RefineCatch Limited, Bungay, Suffolk
Printed and bound by CPI Cox & Wyman, Reading

INTRODUCTION

Why does a Scouser not stare out of the window in the morning?

So he'll have something to do in the afternoon.

Why don't Kopite parents let their sons and daughters marry Evertonians?

Because the kids will be too lazy to steal.

What's got one eye and smells of piss?

Liverpool.

These are the kind of questions that people ask each other over their champagne mojitos, in Manchester, with the kind of enquiry designed to make the Scouser listener feel small and unsure of his or her place in the universe, like, "Do you want people to accept you as you are or do you want them to like you?"

Here are the tales of the good, the bad and the ugly, and that is just the Liverpool midfield. No, the good, the bad and the ugly are as follows, and they do happen in Liverpool.

Good. Your daughter got a new job.

Bad. As a hooker.

Ugly. Your neighbours are her best clients.

Really ugly. She makes more money than you do.

And there are other questions herein, like: How can you tell it is a Scouser looking through a keyhole?

Because you can see both his eyes.

Or: Why was the airport in Liverpool named after John Lennon?

Because that's the first place he went when he made a bit of money.

This is how the Mancs see the Scousers. No stars rising there, as it is West rather than East, so no wise men, just workshy junkies with an attitude problem and bad breath, but their sparky humour means that everything is just hunky-dory.

"Yeh, right," as Mancs say when they mean, "Fuck off."

These are the hits (and misses), the tales tall, true and tautological, that make Mancs laugh. If you can't laugh at Scousers, who can you laugh at?

1

SCOUSERS: CAN'T LIVE WITH THEM, CAN LIVE WITHOUT THEM

Knowsley Park Zoo acquired a very rare species of gorilla. Within a few weeks the gorilla, a female, became very difficult to handle.

Upon examination, the vet determined the problem. The gorilla was in season. To make matters worse, there was no male gorilla available.

Thinking about their problem, the zookeeper thought of Pat Kelly, a Scouser and the part-time worker responsible for cleaning the animal cages.

Pat, like many Scousers, had little sense but possessed ample ability to satisfy a female of any species. The zookeeper thought they might have a solution. Pat was approached with a proposition. Would he be willing to mate with the gorilla for £500? Pat showed some interest, but said he would have to think the matter over carefully.

The following day, he announced that he would accept their offer, but only under four conditions.

"First," Pat said, "I'm not going to kiss her on the lips."

The keeper quickly agreed to this condition.

"Second," he said, "You can tell nobody about this, ever."

The keeper again readily agreed to this.

"Third," Pat said, "I want all the kids raised as Liverpool fans."

Once again it was agreed.

"And last of all," Pat stated, "You're gonna have to give me another week to come up with the £500."

Q. How do you put a twinkle in a Scouser's eye?
A. Shine a torch in his ear.

Why did the Liverpool man climb the glass window?
To see what was on the other side.

How do you save a Scouser from drowning?
Take your foot off his head.

What do hemorrhoids and Scousers have in common?
They're both a complete pain in the arse and never seem to go away completely.

A Scouser won a toilet brush as the booby prize in a raffle. He had never won anything before, though, so he was delighted.

A few weeks later a friend asked if he was getting much use from the toilet brush.

"Well," came the reply, "I don't think much of it. I think I'll go back to using toilet paper."

Scouser hating is not new. This tale is from the 19th century:

A Manchester man detested the Scousers. He griped to his friend: "They're always intoxicated, they never have work, and when they do it's always a shady enterprise."

One day while walking down a street in Liverpool together, they saw a Scouser with an organ grinder at the corner, plying his trade. As they walked pass, the man reached into his pocket, pulled out a guinea, and put it in the monkey's hat.

The man's friend was surprised and asked, "I thought you hated the Scousers?"

The man replied, "Truly I do, but I feel great compassion for their children."

An American, a Manc, and a Scouser were in a terrible car accident . . .

They were all taken to the same A & E, but all

three of them died before they arrived. Just as they were about to put the toe tag on the American, he stirred and opened his eyes. Astonished, the doctors and nurses present asked him what happened.

"Well," said the American, "I remember the crash, and then there was a beautiful light, and then the Manc, the Scouse and I were standing at the gates of Heaven. St Peter approached us and said that we were all too young to die, and that for a donation of $50, we could return to the earth. So of course I pulled out my wallet and gave him the $50, and the next thing I knew I was back here."

"That's amazing!" said one of the doctors. "But what happened to the other two?"

"Last I saw them," replied the American, "the Manc was haggling over the price and the Scouse was waiting for the government to pay for his."

A Scouser is driving down a country road near Manchester, having managed to nick a car, when he spots a farmer standing in the middle of a huge field of grass. He pulls the car over to the side of the road and notices that the farmer is just standing there, doing nothing, looking at nothing.

The man gets out of the car, walks all the way out

to the farmer and asks him, "Excuse me la', but what are you doing?"

The farmer replies, "I'm trying to win a Nobel Prize."

"How?" asks the man, puzzled.

"Well, I heard they give the Nobel Prize to people who are out standing in their field."

If you saw a Scouse lawyer drowning in the Mersey, would you go to lunch or to a movie?

The Archbishop of Canterbury has almost got his way. Liverpool weather has been declared Muslim.

It's partly Sunni but mostly Shi'ite.

There are so many boarded-up houses in Liverpool, that the window cleaner goes round with a sander.

Why do pigeons fly upside down in Liverpool?

Because there's nothing worth shitting on.

2
ANTI-SCOUSER RANT

Here is a man with opinions, none of them positive, about Liverpool.

I am a "Manc" – or should I say a person from Manchester? I recently finished working in Liverpool after 6 years and have now got a job back in Deansgate. I have first-hand experience of Scousers' weird mentality and their belief either that they are always persecuted by the government or that everyone outside their town is out to get them.

A period of mourning would last approximately a couple of months in most cities, however in Liverpool it lasts approximately 50 times as long. This is because, to use the Boris Johnson term they are all "hooked on grief".

For example, most Scousers bleat on about Hillsborough still. Yes, it was a nasty disaster and a great loss but it happened in 1989, yet you still get professional Scousers going on about it all the time like it happened last month. I asked what "Justice for the 96" was and asked how they would still get justice after 20 years. I wished I hadn't – I got lots of dirty looks, threats and loads of "Yer don't know what yer talkin about yer fuckin Manc" retorts. Hutus and Tutsis got over the 1994 Rwandan geno-cide quicker than Scousers got over this and the genocide wasn't an accident. Then there is James Bulger, nearly every 12 to 18 months you get his Mum on the TV moaning about his death in 1993. Yes, it was bad, but get over it, you don't get the par-ents of Ian Huntley's victims whingeing about it every six months.

The best ever thing that showed that they are hooked on grief was when someone found a chicken foetus in an alleyway and the grievers put flowers there, instantly assuming it was a dead baby!

They cannot get over things: Stan Boardman still goes on about the Germans, most Evertonians still blame Liverpool fans for getting them banned out of Europe and most still boycott the Sun news-paper – you aren't Scouse if you read this paper, it's a rule.

There was a car crash on the Formby bypass last month where a scumbag burgled a house in Freshfield and stole a Mercedes car. He crashed it because he couldn't control the car. Another less scumbag off the planet you'd think, no, Scousers have some warped mentality of thieves' honour, they put football shirts and flowers there condoning what he did.

When local gangsters get shot their mates or scared enemies put glowing tributes to them in the Echo pages saying how nice they were, even though they've been stealing since they could crawl and shooting people they never liked the look of.

Most Scousers seem to have 'amusing' anecdotes of robbing things – it must be in your blood, you are born to rob things. We played a game of football up on Mather Avenue and had our entire possessions and coach picked off within six to seven minutes. Don't ever park your car in Liverpool, you'll never see it again!

Whenever I have been on holiday, the loudest person in the room is a Scouser. They have some tribal instinct that needs them to show the whole world where they are from. "Yer know, I'm from Liverpool like, where the Beatles are from yer know." Most think that this will get them a free meal or a round of drinks in Tenerife/Benidorm etc, but the locals haven't got a clue what the hell they are going on about.

Liverpool has an unbelievable amount of professional Scouse celebrities who all profess to be from the "Scottie Road", a slum in the 60s, now just one dead road with a few crap shops on it. Cilla Black, Ricky Tomlinson, Stan Boardman etc – this is a "know yer roots" ploy – one that Scousers seem to be so keen on showing.

A night out in Liverpool, ahhh. Well, you have Mathew Street, populated by crap Beatles themed bars and old over the hill slappers on the pull in places like Boogie Nights, Rubber Soul and Flares. Truly awful places that are always overcrowded, they are also populated by Irish lads who know that most Liverpool women are easy meat. There are also pretentious places like the Living Room, Vampire Lounge, Alma De Cuba where all the women in there are sunbed freaks, wear nothing, love themselves and are out on the pull simply to shag a footballer.

One of my mates had a Spanish friend who came over to visit him and they went to the Blue Bar in Albert Dock. He managed to convince two slappers that he was a Spanish footballer and my mate said he was his agent, in Liverpool to sign for them the next day. They took both of the women back to the hotel room, however they threw the table lamp at the men upon leaving once they had revealed their real jobs – a barber and a waiter.

The city centre is grim and the council are bigger chavs than the population, knocking back decent proposals and replacing them with tasteless shite. Apparently this is also a Manchester conspiracy because the NWDA and English Heritage are based in Manchester and are constantly meddling in their affairs. The pavements in Liverpool are completely splattered with chewing gum and littered with dog shit and MacDonald's wrappers.

The fashion of Liverpool mainly consists of items bought in JJB, Open and until recently Wade Smith – all of it is sports wear of course. There you have it – Liverpool a large city with a small narrow-minded mentality and hooked on grief and negative energy. Roll on 2010.

3

SCOUSERS AND GOD

A train hits a bus filled with Scouser schoolgirls and they all perish.

They are in heaven trying to enter the pearly gates when St Peter asks the first girl, "Tiffany-Jane, have you ever had any contact with a male organ?"

She giggles and shyly replies, "Well, I once touched the head of one with the tip of my finger."

St Peter says, "Okay, dip the tip of your finger in the Holy Water and pass through the gate."

St Peter asks the next girl the same question, "Marie Therese, have you ever had any contact with a male organ?"

The girl is a little reluctant but replies, "Well, once I fondled and stroked one."

St Peter says, "All right, dip your whole hand in the Holy Water and pass through the gate."

All of a sudden, there is a commotion in the line of girls. One girl is pushing her way to the front of the queue. When she reaches the front, St Peter says, "Bernadette, what seems to be the rush?"

The girl replies, "If I'm going to have to gargle that Holy Water, I want to do it before Jessica sticks her arse in it."

So there's a Scotsman, an Irishman and a Liverpudlian sitting in a bar. Jesus Christ walks in and they all feel the need to get him a drink, so they all get a round in for him, and Jesus walks over and says: "Thank you, that was very nice of you."

He puts his hands on the Scotsman's shoulder and all of a sudden the Scotsman's arthritis is cured.

He then puts his hands on the Irishman's shoulders and his cancer is cured.

He then walks over to the Liverpudlian, who screams: "Fuck off! I'm on benefit!"

On the seventh day, God said: "Let there be football."

And it was good.

Later that day, God said: "Let there be one team to rule the others and set the standard for excellence."

With that, he plucked a star from the heavens and placed it on the helmet of red.

God said, "Let it be called Liverpool."

Later that day, God said, "Even football teams need bastards."

So he made their fans.

Three men are to be executed in France: an Evertonian, a Mancunian and a Liverpudlian. They are each asked which way they would like to face before the guillotine is released.

The Evertonian says: "I would like to face the sky so I go to heaven."

So in he goes, the blade is released and it stops an inch from his neck.

The crowd shout: "God has spoken! Let him roam free!" So he is set free.

Then the Mancunian says, "I believe I came from the Earth, so I will face down so I go back."

In he goes, the blade is released and it stops an inch from his neck.

The crowd shout: "God has spoken! Let him roam free!" So off he goes.

Then the Liverpudlian is asked which way he wants to face.

He looks astonished as he says: "Are you crazy? I'm not getting in that thing 'till it's fixed."

What's the difference between Steven Gerrard and God?

God doesn't think he's Steven Gerrard.

4

DEATH AND MARRIAGE

A Liverpool man was placed in intensive care, needles stuck everywhere, tubes running over his disease-ridden body like a spider's web, nearly comatose. A week later, a second man, a Mancunian, was put in the same room in very nearly the same condition.

Both men lay there, near death, machines pinging, oxygen tubes puffing, monitors ding-donging, lights flashing. After a few days, one of the men summoned the strength to weakly raise his hand and catch the other man's attention. He pointed to himself and wheezed out, "Jim."

The other man weakly pointed to himself and said, "Paddy."

This act tired them both out so badly it was another day or two before they had the strength to try again. The first man weakly pointed to himself and murmured in almost inaudible tones: "Liverpool."

The second man replied: "Manchester."

Again the fatigue set in and they both fell fast

asleep. In another couple of days they were at it again.

Jim took several deep breaths, then summoned up the strength to cough out: "Toxteth."

Paddy whispered back: "Moss Side."

This time they were both a little stronger and could continue.

"Cancer," said Jim.

"Sagittarius," replied Paddy.

A newlywed couple, man a Scouser, wife a Manc, had only been married for two weeks. The husband, although very much in love, couldn't wait to go out on the town and for a beer with his old pals.

He said to his new wife, "Darling one, I'll be right back."

"Where are you going, sweetness?" asked the wife.

"I'm going to the bar, pretty face. I'm going to have a beer."

The wife said, "You want a beer, my love?"

She went and opened the fridge door and showed him 25 different kinds of beer brands from 12 different countries: Germany, Holland, Japan, India, etc.

The husband didn't know what to do, and the only thing that he could think of saying was: "Yes, lollipop . . . but at the bar . . . you know . . . they have frozen glasses . . ."

He didn't get to finish the sentence, because the wife interrupted him, saying: "You want a frozen glass, light of my life?"

She then took a huge beer mug out of the freezer, so frozen that she was getting chills just holding it.

The husband, looking a bit pale, said, "Yes, butter-cup, but at the pub they have those hors d'oeuvres that are really delicious. I won't be long, I'll be right back. I promise. OK?"

"You want hors d'oeuvres, poochy pooh?" She opened the oven and took out five different hors d'oeuvres: chicken wings, pigs in blankets, pakora, olives.

"But my sweet, at the pub, you know, there's swearing, dirty words and all that."

"You want dirty words, you Scouse prick? Drink your fucking beer in your fucking frozen mug and eat your fucking snacks, because you are married to me now, and you aren't fucking going anywhere! Got it, arsehole?"

So he stayed home. . .

. . . and they lived happily ever after.

Yeh ri'.

An elderly couple were about to get married. He's from Manchester, she's from Liverpool.

She said, "I want to keep my house."

He said, "That's fine with me."

She said, "And I want to keep my Mercedes."

He said, "That's fine with me."

She said, "And I want to have sex six times a week."

He said, "That's fine with me. Put me down for Friday."

5

DUMB AND DUMBER

A Toxteth carpet installer, yes, the one with the job, decides to take a cigarette break after completing the installation in the first of several rooms in the Manc mansion he has to do. They are not in his pocket so he begins searching, only to notice a small lump in his recently completed carpet installation. Not wanting to rip up all that work for a packet of fags he simply walks over with his lump hammer and pounds the lump flat. He decides to forgo the break and continues on to the other rooms to be carpeted.

At the end of the day he's completed his work and is loading his tools into his van when two events occur almost simultaneously. He spies his packet of cigarettes on the dashboard of the van, and the lady of the house calls out, "Excuse me, have you seen my budgie?"

A blonde walks into a chemist in Liverpool and asks the assistant for some rectum deodorant.

The pharmacist, a little bemused, explains to the woman that they don't sell rectum deodorant and never have.

The blonde assures the pharmacist that she has been buying the stuff from this shop on a regular basis and would like some more.

"I'm sorry," says the chemist, "We don't have any."

"But, I always buy it here," says the blonde.

"Do you have the container that it came in?" asks the pharmacist.

"Yes," said the blonde, "I'll go home and get it."

She returns with the container and hands it to the pharmacist who looks at it and says to her, "This is just a normal stick of underarm deodorant."

Annoyed, the blonde snatches the container back and reads out loud from the container. "To apply, push up bottom."

A new report from Liverpool University suggests that being overweight in Scally City is not as harmful as is commonly believed, and actually confers some surprising benefits.

Being five to ten pounds overweight could protect people from ailments ranging from tuberculosis to Alzheimer's disease, research indicates. Those carrying 15 to 25 extra pounds are better able to recover from adverse conditions such as emphysema, pneumonia, and various injuries and infections, states the report.

Thirty to 40 pounds of flab could help fend off breast, kidney, pancreatic, prostate, and colon cancer. And an extra 50 pounds on the scale may improve eyesight, reverse baldness, cure the common cold, and reduce global warming.

In general, the report concludes, overweight people are happier, more successful in business, cleverer, and friendlier.

The study was funded by a research grant from Greigs, McDonald's, Burger King, Domino's Pizza, Starbucks and Haagen Daz.

Scouse New Year Resolutions.
1. Read less.
2. I want to gain weight. Put on at least three stones.
3. Stop exercising. Waste of time.
4. Watch more TV. I've been missing some good stuff.
5. Procrastinate more. Or put it off.
6. Drink. Lots and lots.
7. Start being superstitious.
8. Spend less time at work.
9. Stop bringing lunch from home. I should eat out more.
10. Take up a new habit. Maybe smoking.

A recent study by Liverpool University claims that elderly Scousers who drink beer or wine at least four times a week have the highest bone density.

The report goes on to say that they need that extra bone density, as they are the ones falling down the most.

A cab picks up a Scouse nun in Manchester city centre. She gets into the cab, and notices that the very handsome cab driver won't stop staring at her. She asks him why he is staring. He replies, "I have a question to ask you, but I don't want to offend you, even if that is a Scouse accent."

She answers, "My son, you cannot offend me. When you're as old as I am and have been a nun as long as I have, you get a chance to see and hear just about everything. I'm sure that there's nothing you could say or ask that I would find offensive."

The taxi driver says, "Well, I've always had a fantasy to have a nun kiss me."

She responds, "Let's see what we can do about that. Number one, you have to be single and number two, you must be Catholic."

The cab driver is very excited and says, "Yes, I'm single and Catholic."

"OK," the nun says. "Pull into the next side street."

The nun fulfills his fantasy, with a kiss that would make a hooker blush, but when they get back on the road, the cab driver starts crying.

"My dear child," says the nun, "why are you crying?"

"Forgive me, but I've sinned. I lied and I must confess. I'm married and I'm Church of England."

The nun says, "That's OK. My name's Kevin and I'm going to a fancy dress party."

One day two Scousers were doing a crossword.

Jack turns to Mick and says, "Old McDonald had one of these."

"Hey, I know," says Mick. "It's got to be a farm."

"How do you spell that?" asks Jack.

"E-I-E-I-O," says Mick.

What's the difference between a Scouser and a chimp?

One's hairy, stupid and smells, and the other is a chimpanzee.

6

RETIREMENT CAN BE FUN

A Manc octogenarian, who was an avid golfer, moved to Liverpool and joined the local club, Allerton Manor. He went to the club for the first time to play, but he was told there wasn't anyone with whom he could play because they were already out on the course. He repeated several times that he really wanted to play. Finally, the assistant pro said he would play with him and asked how many strokes he wanted for a bet. The 80-year-old said, "I really don't need any strokes, because I have been playing quite well. The only real problem I have is getting out of bunkers."

And he did play well. Coming to the par four eighteenth they were even. The pro had a nice drive and was able to get on the green and a two-putt for a par. The old man had a good drive, but his approach shot landed in a bunker next to the green. Playing from the bunker, he hit a high ball which landed on the green and rolled into the hole. Birdie, match and all the money, yeehah. The pro walked over to the bunker where his opponent was still standing.

He said, "Nice shot, but I thought you said you have a problem getting out of bunkers?"

Replied the octogenarian, "I do. Please give me a hand."

Working people frequently ask retired Mancs what they do to make their days interesting.

Me, I went to Liverpool the other day and I went for a beer.

I was only in the pub for about five minutes, but when I came out there was a parking attendant writing out a parking ticket, so I went up to him and said, "Come on, pal, how about giving an old guy a break?"

He ignored me and continued writing. I called him a Nazi. He glared at me and started writing another for having worn tyres. So I called him a shitbag. He finished the second ticket and put it on the windscreen with the first. Then he started writing a third and fourth ticket for further faults he kept finding.

This went on for about 20 minutes. The more I abused him, the more tickets he wrote.

I didn't give a monkey's, because I came on the train.

7

POETRY CORNER

Manchester Ladies' Poem

Before I lay me down to sleep,
I pray for a man, who's not a creep,
One who's handsome, smart and strong.
One who loves to listen long,
One who thinks before he speaks,
One who'll ring, not wait for weeks.
I pray he's gainfully employed,
When I spend his dosh, won't be annoyed.
Pulls out my chair and opens my door,
Massages my back and begs to do more.
Oh! Send me a man who'll make love to my mind,
Knows what to answer to 'how big is my behind?'
One who'll make love till my body's itchin',
And brings ME a sandwich too
When he goes to the kitchen.
I pray that this man will love me no end,
And never compare me to my best friend.
Thank you in advance and now I'll just wait,
For I know you will send him before it's too late.

Liverpool Ladies Poem

He didn't like my casserole
And he didn't like my cake.
He said my biscuits were too hard . . .
Not like his mother used to make.

I didn't make the coffee right
He didn't like the stew,
I didn't mend his socks
The way his mother used to do.

I pondered for an answer
I was looking for a clue.
Then I kicked the shit out of him.

Manchester Poem: The Perfect Man

The perfect man is gentle
Never cruel or mean
He has a beautiful smile
And he keeps his face so clean.

The perfect man likes children
And will raise them by your side
He will be a good father
As well as a good husband to his bride.

The perfect man loves cooking
Cleaning and vacuuming too
He'll do anything in his power
To convey his feelings of love for you.

The perfect man is sweet
Making poetry from your name
He's a best friend to your mother
And kisses away your pain.

He has never made you cry
Or hurt you in any way
Oh, fuck this stupid poem
The perfect man is gay.

A Liverpool Love Poem

Of course I love yer darling
You're a crackin' top notch berd
And when I say you're gorgeous
I mean every single werd

So yer bum is on the big side
I don't mind a bit of flab
It means that when I'm ready
There's somethin' there to grab

So your belly isn't flat no more
I tell yer, I don't care
So long as when I cuddle yer
I can get my arms round there

No woman who is your age
Has nice round perky breasts
They just gave in to gravity
But I know yer did yer best

I'm tellin' yer the truth now
I never tell yer lies
I think it's very sexy
That you've got dimples on yer thighs

I swear on ma granny's grave now
The moment that we met
I thought you were as good as
I was ever gonna get

No matter what ye look like
I'll always love yer dear
Now shut up while the footy's on
And get me another beer.

Scouse Guy's Free Verse

I pray for a deaf-mute nymphomaniac with huge boobs who owns a pub and two seats in the Directors' Box at Anfield.

This doesn't rhyme and I don't give a fuck.

8

OUT OF THE MOUTHS OF KIDS

A three-year-old Bootle boy examined his penis and scrotum while taking a bath.

"Mum," he asked, "Are these my brains?"

"Not yet," she replied.

A fireman near Dingle is working outside the station when he notices a little Dingle girl in a little red cart with tiny ladders on the sides and a garden hose coiled in the middle. She is wearing a yellow plastic fireman's helmet. The cart is being pulled by her dog and her cat.

"That is a nice fire engine," the fireman says with admiration.

"Thanks," the girl says.

The fire fighter takes a closer look and notices the girl has tied the cart to her dog's collar and to the cat's testicles.

"Little one," the fireman says, "I don't want to tell you how to run your own engine, but if you were to tie that rope around the cat's collar, I think you could go faster."

The little girl replies thoughtfully, "You're probably right, but then I wouldn't have a siren."

A Scouser in a white car pulls up to a kid and says: "Get in the car and I'll give you a tenner."

Kid says no and walks on.

Man says: "Get in the car and I'll give you twenty quid."

Kid says no and walks on.

Man says: "Come on kid, get in the car and I'll give you fifty quid."

Kid says: "For the last time, Dad, I'm not gonna be seen in a fucking Skoda."

Teacher to class: "What does your daddy do at weekends?"

Little boy: "He's a dancer in a gay bar."

Teacher takes him outside and asks, "Is this true?"

"No miss, it's bollocks," he replies. "He plays for Liverpool, but I was too embarrassed to say that."

It was that time, during the Liverpool Sunday morning service, for the children's sermon. All the children were invited to come forward.

One little girl was wearing a particularly pretty dress and, as she sat down, the minister leaned over and said: "That is a very pretty dress. Is it your Easter Dress?"

The little girl replied, directly into the minister's clip-on microphone, "Yes, and my Mum says it's a right bastard to iron."

A little boy took his parents to court because he did not want to live with them anymore. The honoured judge said to him, "So why don't you want to live with your dad?"

"Because he beats me," said the little boy.

"Why don't you want to live with your mum then?" asked the judge.

"Because she beats me as well."

"Oh," said the judge. "Well who would you like to live with then?"

The little boy replied, "I would like to live with Liverpool FC, because they don't beat anyone."

9

GOOD ADVICE AND OBSERVATIONS

Support bacteria. They're the only culture some Scousers have.

Scousers are like laxatives. They irritate the shit out of you.

Scousers are like weather. Nothing can be done to change them.

Scousers are like insurance policies. They take soooooooo long to mature.

Scousers are like mascara. They usually run at the first sign of emotion.

Scousers are like lava lamps. Fun to look at, but not very bright.

Some general musings for Mancs:

If at first you don't succeed, skydiving is not for you.

Life is sexually transmitted.

Good health is merely the slowest possible rate at which one can die.

Men have two emotions: hungry and horny. If you see him without an erection, make him a sandwich.

Give a Liverpudlian a fish and you feed them for a day. Teach them to use the internet and they won't bother you for weeks.

Some Liverpool people are like a Slinky. Not really good for anything, but you still can't help but smile when you shove them down the stairs.

Health freaks are going to feel stupid some day, lying in hospitals dying of nothing.

All of us could take a lesson from the weather. It pays no attention to criticism.

Why does a slight tax increase cost you £200.00 and a substantial tax cut saves you £30.00?

In the 60s, people took acid to make the world weird. Now the world is weird and people take Prozac to make it normal.

Save the whales. Collect the whole set.

42.7 percent of all statistics are made up on the spot. Not this one, though, oh no.

Over 99 percent of Liverpool lawyers give the rest a bad name.

I feel like I'm diagonally parked in a parallel universe.

Honk if you love peace and quiet.

Remember, half the people you know are below average.

The early bird may get the worm, but the second mouse gets the cheese.

Monday is an awful way to spend 1/7 of your week.

A clear conscience is usually the sign of a bad memory.

Plan to be spontaneous tomorrow.

Always try to be modest, and be proud of it.

If you think nobody cares, try missing a couple of payments.

How many of you believe in psycho-kinesis? Raise my hand.

OK, so what's the speed of dark?

How do you tell when you're out of invisible ink?

If everything seems to be going well, you have obviously overlooked something.

When everything is coming your way, you're in the wrong lane.

If Barbie is so popular, why do you have to buy her friends?

Eagles may soar, but weasels don't get sucked into jet engines.

What happens if you get scared half to death twice?

I used to have an open mind but my brains kept falling out.

Why do psychics have to ask you for your name?

Inside every older person is a younger person wondering what the fuck happened.

Just remember – if the world didn't suck, we would all fall off.

Life in Liverpool isn't about how to survive the storm, but how to dance in the rain.

Golf club no women rule. That's as in no women except those under 25 with big tits.

If you can't fix it with a hammer, it's an electrical problem.

And remember.
  Life is like a roll of toilet paper.
  The closer it gets to the end, the faster it goes.

10

IF YOU HATE SCOUSERS CLAP YOUR HANDS. CLAP CLAP CLAP.

I was checking into a hotel the other week. At the counter, the Scouser in front of me said curtly to the receptionist, "I hope the porn channel is disabled."

Unbelievable what some people are into.

I asked a guy: "Where are you from?"
    He replied: "Liverpool."
    I said: "Sorry."
    He repeated: "Liverpool."
    "No, I heard you," I said. "I'm just sorry."

What do you call a Liverpudlian?
    A dirty murdererin' bastard.
    That's not a joke, just needed saying like.

A Scouser got caught shagging corpses.
    Some rotten bastard split on him.

Scouser says to his mate Mick: "I'm shagging twins at the moment."

Mick asks: "How can you tell the difference?"

The Scouser says: "Her brother's got a moustache."

What do you get if you cross a monkey with a Liverpudlian?

Nothing. Monkeys are far too clever to screw a Liverpudlian.

How many Scousers does it take to change a light bulb?

When they get electricty I'll let you know!

Why can't you circumcise a Kopite?

Because there is no end to those pricks.

A bomb went off in Tesco killing ten Liverpudlians.

Tesco: every little helps.

A farmer from Barnsley catches a Scouser drinking from his stream and shouts, "Heyop cock, ya don't wanna be drinking water from there. It's full of horse piss, cow shit and the overflow from our cess pit."

The Scouser replies, "I'm from Liverpool, mate, and didn't catch what ya said, can you speak a bit slower?"

"Sure," replies the farmer, "if you use two hands you'll be able to drink much quicker."

I'm fucking gutted. I've just been told there's a Scouser in our family tree. Mind you, I've just looked out my bedroom window and have to admit that he does look fucking good hanging there.

Why do Scousers smell?

So blind people can hate them too.

11

SCOUSE WOMEN

What's the difference between Scouse women and the male race?

Scouse women have a higher sperm count.

What do Scouse women use for sexual protection?

A bus shelter.

Why do Scouse women wear knickers?

To keep their ankles warm.

A man walks into a shop in Liverpool: "Can I have a pair of tights for my wife?"

Shop assistant: "Certainly sir, what size head are you?"

Why do Sumo wrestlers shave their legs?

So they're not mistaken for Liverpudlian women.

How long does it take a Scouse girl to have a shit?
  About nine months.

A girl from Anfield writes to a problem page: "Dear Anna, I'm 13 years old and still a virgin. Do you think my brothers are gay?"

75 percent of 14-year-old girls in Liverpool admit to regularly going out binge drinking. Who the hell is looking after their kids?

12

LAZY, LYIN', THIEVIN' BASTARDS

What's the difference between a Scouser and a mutual fund?

The mutual fund eventually matures and earns money.

"Gentlemen of the jury," shouted the crier in a Liverpool court, "please proceed to your accustomed places."

The court erupted as the 12 scallies proceeded to cram themselves into the dock.

Which is the odd one out, a cow, a tragedy and the welfare state?

The cow, it's the only one a Scouser can't milk.

What's long, Scouse and goes round corners?

The dole queue.

Scouser: "I went for a job interview at the Samaritans yesterday."

Manc: "Did you get it?"

Scouser: "Nah, the bastards talked me out of it."

Scouse fella takes a woman home from a nightclub.

She says to him, rubbing his cock: "Mmmm, show me it's true what they say about men from Liverpool."

So he stabbed her and nicked her handbag.

What's the highest mountain in Liverpool called?

Kill a man for a giro.

Liverpool have signed a new Japanese player.

Nicamotor.

How do you know when you have been burgled by a Scouser?

The bins are empty and the dog's pregnant.

What should you do if you see a Scouser jogging?

Trip him up and give the lady's purse back to her.

How do you make a Scouser run faster?

Stick a plasma telly under his arm.

What do you say to a Scouser in uniform?
Will the defendant please rise?

Latest news reports advise that a cell of four terrorists has been operating in Merseyside, Liverpool.
Police advised earlier today that three of the four
have been detained. The Merseyside Regional Police
Commissioner stated that the terrorists Bin
Thievin, Bin Drinkin and Bin Fightin have been
arrested on immigration issues.

The Police advise further that they can find no
one fitting the description of the fourth cell member, Bin Workin, in the area. Police are confident
that anyone who looks like Bin Workin will be very
easy to spot in the community.

Scouse bloke walks in to the job centre and says to
the fella behind the desk, "Gorra job, la?"

The Job Centre assistant replies: "Yes. As a
matter of fact, we have something that has only just
come in. We have a billionaire oil baron who wants
someone to be a Personal Assistant to his 18-year-
old, blonde glamour-model daughter. You will be
responsible for her modelling assignments, her lingerie purchases and you will be expected to accompany her 24 hours a day. You will also be expected to

drive her around in a brand new Bentley. You will have your own private annexe to the mansion and you will live rent free with a yearly salary of £250,000."

The Scouse fella looks at the assistant in amazement and says, "Thass bullshit, la!"

To which the assistant replied, "Well, you fucking started it."

Liverpool airport has been shut for the past eight hours due to a 'suspicious car'. Apparently it had tax, insurance and the radio was still in it.

A poll asked a thousand Scousers if Britain should change it's currency to the Euro.

99 percent of them disagreed and said that they would prefer to keep the Giro.

A Scouser is driving through Liverpool with his dog in the passenger seat. A police panda car follows him for about half a mile and then puts its siren and stop sign on indicating to him to pull over. As the copper approaches the car he sees the Scouser is slapping the dog's head.

He tells the driver to wind down his window and asks, "Why are you hitting the dog?"

The Scouser replies, "The bloody thing just ate my tax disc."

I bought a Liverpool advent calendar.

All the windows were boarded up and the chocolates had been nicked.

Freezing temperatures in Liverpool this morning.

Reports say it was so cold a Scouser was seen with his hands in his own pockets.

13

LIVERPOOL ARE SHITE

Liverpool manager Rafael Benitez walked into the Nationwide Building Society one day while a robbery was in progress. One of the robbers hit him over the head and knocked Rafa out.

Whilst coming around, he said "Jesus, where the hell am I?"

One of the staff told him he was in the Nationwide.

Benitez replied: "It's May already then."

What's the difference between Liverpool and an albatross?

An albatross has got two decent wings.

Why do Scousers put football kits on their kids?

If they get shot, they get to meet the team.

British Rail have decided to start sponsoring Liverpool.

The company think they are a suitable team because of their regular points failures.

How can you tell ET is a Liverpool fan?
Because he looks like one.

A Liverpool supporter goes to his doctor to find out what's wrong with him.
"Your problem is you're fat," says the doctor.
"I'd like a second opinion," responds the man.
"OK, you're ugly too," replies the doctor.

Four surgeons are taking a tea break:
The first surgeon says, "Accountants are the best to operate on because when you open them up, everything inside is numbered."
The second surgeon says, "Nope, librarians are the best. Everything inside them is in alphabetical order."
The third surgeon says, "Well you should try electricians. Everything inside them is colour coded."
The fourth surgeon says, "I prefer Liverpool fans. They're heartless, spineless, gutless and their heads and arses are interchangeable."

Unsubstantiated reports seem to suggest that Liverpool will be releasing a new record at the end of the month: 'I'm Forever Blowing Doubles'.

How many Liverpool fans can you get in a police car?

One in the front, two in the back, and one on top going: "nee naw neee naww neee naw."

What happens when Man U cross the halfway line at Anfield?

They score.

How many Liverpool fans does it take to change a lightbulb?

None – they're quite happy living in the shadows.

A Man U fan and a Scouser are strolling along the street and suddenly the Man U supporter says, "Woooh! Would ya look at that dead bird!"

The Liverpool fan looks skywards and says: "Huh, Where?"

How many Liverpool fans does it take to change a light bulb?

As many as you like, but they'll never see the light.

What do you call all the Liverpool fans on the moon?
Problem solved.

What do you call a Liverpool fan with an IQ of 10?
Supremely gifted!

If a male Liverpool fan divorces his wife do they still remain brother and sister?

What happens when Liverpool win the Premier?
They turn off the playstation.

Does anyone know how to fix a sat-nav?
My one's broken. It keeps saying Liverpool are still in Europe.

A Liverpool fan got caught shagging biscuits.
He was fucking crackers.

Liverpool fans sing 'You'll Never Walk Alone' because none of them own a car.

If a small condom goes on a small prick, and a medium sized one goes on a medium sized prick, what goes on a big prick?

A Liverpool shirt.

Three Liverpool fans in a mini drive off the end of a cliff. Why is it a shame?

A mini has four seats.

Two Liverpool fans race each other in the London marathon. Half way round they both have heart attacks and die. Who wins?

Society.

Apparently Liverpool have got a rare cross virus of swine and bird flu which will prevent them winning the Premiership.

It's called 'Pigs might fucking fly' flu.

Why are Liverpool supporters terrible at making pancakes?

Because they're all useless tossers.

A Liverpool fan walks past a shop and sees the video 'Liverpool – The Glory Years'. He goes into the shop and asks how much.

"£100," says the shopkeeper.

"That's a bit steep, how come it's so dear?"

"Well, it's a tenner for the video and £90 for the Betamax recorder."

Rafael Benitez: "Our new winger cost 15 million. I call him our wonder player."

Sir Alex Ferguson: "Why's that?"

Rafael Benitez: "Every time he plays I wonder why I bothered to buy him!"

What's is the difference between Pamela Anderson and the Liverpool goal?

Pam's only got two tits in front of her.

What do Liverpool fans and mushrooms have in common?

They both have big heads and live in shit.

Alex Ferguson is at a charity dinner when a gorgeous girl comes and asks for his autograph.

Unfortunately she hasn't got any paper so she says: "Why don't you come up to my room and you can sign my bum?"

To which Fergie replies: "Sorry love, but Rafa signs all the bums."

Why does Rafa Benitez keep visiting Argos?

Because that's the only way he can pick up any Premier points.

A girl at work approached me the other day to say she was worried about hearing voices. We went somewhere quiet where I too started hearing voices. It appeared to be coming from between her legs so I knelt down by her crotch and listened.

"Liverpool are gonna win the league," the voice said.

The girl said in a panic, "Did you hear that? What do you think I should do?"

I replied, "Don't worry love, a lot of fannies talk like this."

I was DJ-ing at a Liverpool FC player's wedding the other day. During the speeches, for a laugh, I decided to toast the happy couple.

The guests didn't see the funny side and neither did the fucking fire brigade!!

What's the difference between a Liverpool fan and a broken clock?

Even a broken clock is right twice a day!

Three football fans were driving along when they spied a body in the undergrowth. Stopping their car, the three guys ran over to see what they could do. Unfortunately, they found the nude body of a deceased young woman.

Being gentlemen, the first guy dropped his Spurs hat over one breast. The second guy, an Arsenal fan, placed his hat over the other breast. The Liverpool fan then placed his hat over the woman's private parts.

Soon the police arrived. The coroner started checking over the body. He picked up the Spurs hat and quickly placed it back. He then picked up the Arsenal hat and returned it. Then he picked up the Liverpool fan hat, put it down, then picked it up again inspecting the hat more closely, and then put it down. Then he picked it up a third time.

By this time, the Liverpool fan was a bit irritated and he asked, "Why do you keep picking up that hat? Are you some kind of pervert or something?"

The coroner responded with a wry smile, "Son, I can't figure this one out. Usually when I come across one of these Liverpool hats, there's an arsehole under it."

What do you get if you cross a Liverpol fan with a pig?

Thick bacon . . .

How do you make a Liverpool fan run?

Build a job centre.

Why do Liverpool fans plant potatoes round the edge of Anfield?

So that they have something to lift at the end of the season.

You know why Liverpool idiots are always singing "You'll never walk alone"??

It's because there are two other clubs accompanying them when they get bloody relegated.

Rafa Benitez was wheeling his shopping trolley across the supermarket car park when he noticed an old lady struggling with her shopping.

He stopped and asked: "Can you manage, dear?" to which the old lady replied, "No way. You got yourself into this mess. Don't ask me to sort it out."

A female Liverpool fan goes up to Benitez and says, "Hi Rafa, will you autograph my pussy for me?"

"Fuck off," he replies, "I've signed more than enough twats since I've been here."

Three Liverpool supporters were in a pub and spotted a United fan at the bar. The first one said he was going to piss him off. He walked over to the United fan and tapped him on the shoulder.

"Hey Manc, I hear your Rio Ferdinand is a poof."

"Really? I didn't know that."

Puzzled, the Scouser walked back to his buddies.

"I told him Ferdinand was a poof and he didn't care."

"You just don't know how to set him off, watch and learn."

The second Scouser walked over and tapped the United fan on the shoulder.

"Hey Manc, I hear your Rio Ferdinand is a transvestite poof!"

"Oh, Christ, I wasn't aware of that, thanks."

Shocked beyond belief, the Scouser went back to his buddies.

"You're right. He is unshakeable!"

The third Scouser said, "No, no, no, I will really piss him off, you just watch."

The Scouser walked over to the United fan, tapped him on the shoulder and said . . .

"Hey Manc, I hear your Rio Ferdinand is a Liverpool supporter!"

"Apparently so. Just as your mates said earlier."

Osama Bin Laden has just made a reportedly live TV appearance. He said: "To prove I am still alive, Liverpool were a bag of shite on Saturday."

The British Government claims that it could have been recorded months ago.

Two Liverpool fans walk into a bar.

You'd think one of them would have seen it.

Liverpool football club have re-arranged their end of season dinner at short notice.

It's now being held tonight.

Fancy going along?

Dress code: 70s and 80s style only!

MENU

STARTER: Sour Grapes.

MAIN COURSE: Plaice (might be 4th).

Free bar – terms and conditions apply – only drinks available are BITTER for the drinkers and BITTER LEMON for the designated drivers, NO DOUBLES OR TREBLES ALLOWED! Drinks will be served in glasses only – no cups currently available.

PUDDING: Selection from Gerrard, Torres, Voronin, Riera etc. A huge choice, including humble pie.

Followed by hard cheese and biscuits

There will also be a fine selection of whines on offer!

Entertainment will be provided by Rafa Benitez doing his party trick of making £200 million disappear into thin air with nothing to show for it!

Man goes to doctor and says: "I have a problem. Every time I masturbate I start to sing 'You'll Never Walk Alone'.

After a few minutes the doctor realises what the problem is, and replies: "Don't worry about it. Lots of wankers sing that."

What would Peter Crouch be if he weren't a Premiership footballer?
A virgin.

A Manchester man walks into a bric-a-brac shop while on holiday and sees an ornamental brass rat, the sort of thing women of a certain age love to put on the mantelpiece. He thinks: "That'll be perfect for me Mother's birthday," so he asks the shopkeeper how much it is.

"£25 for the rat, £100 for the story," replies the man.

"Forget the story," says the bloke, and so buys the rat for 25 quid. He walks off down the road, but has not gone 30 yards when a rat comes up from the gutter and starts to follow him. Soon more arrive, and in a few minutes the whole street is a sea of rats, all following the bloke, who keeps walking until he comes to a cliff. He throws the brass rat over, and millions of rats follow, one after each other, plunging to certain death. The bloke then runs back to the shop.

"Aaaah," says the shopkeeper, "you'll be back for the story."

"Screw the story – do you have a brass Liverpool fan?"

A Leeds fan, a Liverpool fan and a Man U fan were all in Saudi Arabia, sharing a smuggled crate of booze. All of a sudden the Saudi police rushed in and arrested them. The mere possession of alcohol is a severe offence in Saudi Arabia, so for the terrible crime of actually being caught consuming the booze, they were sentenced to death.

However, after many months and with the help of very good lawyers, they were able to successfully appeal their sentence down to life imprisonment.

By a stroke of luck, it was a Saudi national holiday the day their trial finished, and the extremely benevolent Sheikh decided they could be released after receiving just 20 lashes each of the whip.

As they were preparing for their punishment, the Sheikh suddenly said: "It's my first wife's birthday today, and she has asked me to allow each of you one wish before your whipping."

The Leeds fan was first in line (he had drunk the least), so he thought about this for a while and then said: "Please tie a pillow to my back." This was done, but the pillow only lasted 10 lashes before the whip went through. The Leeds fan had to be carried away bleeding and crying with pain when the punishment was done.

The Scouser was next up and after watching the scene, said: "Please fix two pillows on my back, under my dress" But even two pillows and one dress could only take 15 lashes before the whip went through again.

The Manc was the last one up (he had finished off the crate), but before he could say anything, the

Sheikh turned to him and said: "You are from a most beautiful part of the world, your city has some of the best bars, nightclubs and restaurants in Europe, your city and football team is known throughout the world. For this, you may have two wishes!"

"Ta mate, your Most Royal and Merciful Highness," the Manc replies. "In recognition of your kindness, my first wish is that you give me not 20, but 100 lashes."

"Not only are you an honourable, handsome and powerful man, you are also very brave," the Sheik says with an admiring look on his face. "If 100 lashes is what you desire, then so be it. And your second wish? What is it to be?" the Sheikh asks.

"Please tie the Scouser to my back."

Do you know when Liverpool will become EPL champions?

On February 30.

What ship has never docked in Liverpool?

The Premiership . . . wahaaaaaaaaaaaa.

Steven Gerrard walks into a sperm donor bank.

"I'd like to donate some sperm," he says to the receptionist.

"Certainly Sir," replies the receptionist, "have you donated before?"

"Yes," replies Gerrard, "you should have my details on your computer."

"Oh yes, I've found your details," says the receptionist, "but I see you're going to need help. Shall I call someone to help you?"

"Why do I need help?" asks Gerrard.

The receptionist replies, "Well Steve, it says on your record that you're a useless tosser."

Snow White, Arnold Schwarzenegger and Quasimodo are having a conversation.

Snow White says: "Everybody tells me I am the most beautiful, divine woman that any man has ever laid his eyes on, but how do I know?"

Arnie says: "I know what you mean. Everybody tells me I am the most muscular, hunky man that has ever lived, but how do I know?"

Quasimodo says: "Yes. Everybody tells me I am the most disgusting, despicable, grotesque creature that has ever roamed the earth, but how do I know?"

Snow White says "Let's go and see the wise man!" So off they go.

Snow White goes in first and five minutes later she comes out and says: "It's true. I am the most beautiful, divine woman that any man has ever laid his eyes on."

Arnie goes in and five minutes later he comes out and says: "It's true. I am the most muscular, hunky man that has ever lived."

Quasimodo goes in and five minutes later he comes out and says: "Who's this Rafael Benitez character then?"

14

SIGNS YOU'VE BEEN IN LIVERPOOL TOO LONG

1. You have an urge to steal.

2. You think Brookside was a 'glamorous' soap.

3. You think Hollyoaks is 'posh'.

4. You keep going on about how great Liverpool and Scousers are.

5. You often wonder why so many Scousers leave Liverpool and never come back.

6. To you, organised crime is putting petrol in the getaway car.

7. You start to cry when you hear 'Ferry Cross the Mersey'.

8. You think that Albert Dock is 'for the tourists'. What tourists?

9. You think anyone from Liverpool has a great sense of humour.

10. You often wonder why you don't hear of many Scouse comedians any more.

SCOUSERS

VS.

MANCS

2

SCOUSERS START HERE

First published 2009
by Black & White Publishing Ltd
29 Ocean Drive, Edinburgh EH6 6JL

1 3 5 7 9 10 8 6 4 2   09 10 11 12 13

ISBN: 978 1 84502 277 8

Typeset by RefineCatch Limited, Bungay, Suffolk
Printed and bound by CPI Cox & Wyman, Reading

INTRODUCTION

The 28 percent longer that the people from Manchester live compared to Liverpudlians is all spent talking about the decline in property values, as is the other 72 percent, so what is the point of living longer? A bigger percentage of their kids go to private schools and universities, but most of them are so thick that you could drive nails into them without them noticing and as for any sense of fashion or style, forget it. Manchester buys fashion, Liverpool creates it.

As for the leafy suburban academia, you can stick it where the sun don't shine. Scousers don't hide in big houses and gossip about their neighbours, they gossip about their neighbours in the streets and pubs. And if the gossip does tend to the more physical and leads to the odd stabbing, at least you get stabbed in the front, rather than the mental wounds inflicted by those backstabbing, arrogant snobs of Mancs, most of whom are scared to go near Liverpool without an escort of uniformed, helmeted fascists, aka the police.

And Liverpudlians can and do laugh at themselves. St Jude's Christmas panto for paranoid schizophrenics ended in chaos last night, when someone

shouted, "HE'S BEHIND YOU!" is typical of the black humour that thrives in the 'Pool.

Adversity and deprivation? Bring them on! Liverpool thrives on them. But they don't mess much with Mancunians, as it's not nice to pick on the mentally challenged.

These are the jibes, jabs and gibberings that make the people of Liverpool the salt (and vinegar) of the earth.

1

SLIGHTS AND SNUBS

Item on Liverpool hotel bill for a Manc: Wear and tear on mirror . . . 10 pence.

Two Mancs walk past a bar . . . Well, it could happen.

What's this: X X X?
 Three Mancs co-signing a loan.

What is the difference between Mancs and terrorists?
 Terrorists usually have sympathizers.

You are driving in the town one day, and see a member of the town council and a Manc crossing the road. Which one do you run over first?
 Answer: The councillor. *Always* business before pleasure.

Where's the safest place to hide money from a Manc?
 Under the soap.

Have you heard the one about the Manc who bought an AM radio?

He'd had it two years before he realised he could listen to it in the afternoon.

What do you do if a Manc throws a grenade at you?

Take out the pin and throw it back.

What happens to a girl who goes out with a Manc for the evening?

Nothing.

Did you know that if a Manc moves to Liverpool he decreases the level of intelligence in both cities?

What are the best ten years of a Manc's life?

Primary One.

A note for Mancs: "You can't take it with you, and even if you could if would melt."

A young mixed-marriage (he was a Manc, she was a Scouser) couple left the church and arrived at the hotel where they were spending the first night of their honeymoon. They opened the champagne and began undressing. When the bridegroom removed his socks, his new wife asked, "Ewww, what's wrong

with your feet? Your toes look all mangled and terrible. Why are your feet so ugly?"

"I had tolio as a child," he answered.

"You mean polio?" she asked.

"No, tolio. The disease only affected my toes."

The bride was satisfied with this explanation, and they continued undressing. When the groom took off his trousers, his bride once again wrinkled up her nose.

"What's wrong with your knees?" she asked. "They're all lumpy and deformed."

"As a child, I also had kneasles," he explained.

"You mean measles?" she asked.

"No, kneasles. It was a strange illness that only affected my knees."

The new bride had to be satisfied with this answer. As the undressing continued, her husband at last removed his underwear. She looked down at his member.

"Don't tell me," she said. "Let me guess. Smallcox?"

Being a financially prudent man, Mr. MacLennan the Manc was rather upset when he accidentally let a 50p coin fall into the public toilet.

"What shall I do?" he wondered. "Is it worth delving in there for 50p?" Then he had a brainwave.

Reaching into his pocket, he found another 50p coin and dropped it in too.

"A pound's another matter entirely," he thought, rolling up his sleeve.

As the Murphy twins, separated at birth, Paul Manc and Peter Scouse, sat watching TV, on screen came the Tour de France cycle race.

"Why do they do that?" asked Paul.

"Do what?" said Peter.

"Cycle for miles and miles, up hill, down dale. Month after month, day after day. Through wind, rain, snow, ice. Why do they continually torture themselves?"

"It's because," said Peter, "the winner gets half a million pounds."

"Yes," asked the Manc, "But why do the others do it?"

One morning a Manc was driving through the outskirts of Liverpool.

As he stopped at the light a massive guy stepped into the middle of the road. The man is at least six feet four and has the appearance of a walking wardrobe. The tattoos are welcomed by people because they hide bits of his face. This guy is fearsome.

At the roadside there also stands a young woman.

She is absolutely beautiful – slim, shapely, fair complexion, golden hair . . . heart stopping. The driver stops and stares, and his attention is only distracted from the lovely girl when the thing opens the car door and drags him from his seat onto the road with a fist resembling a whole raw ham.

"Right, you," he shouts. "I want you to masturbate."

"But . . ." stammers the driver.

"Do it now . . . or I'll kill yer!"

So the driver turns his back on the girl, drops his trousers and starts to masturbate. Thinking of the girl on the roadside this doesn't take him long.

"Right!" snarls the Scouser. "Do it again!"

"But . . ." says the driver.

"Now!"

So the driver does it again.

"Right la', do it again," demands the monster.

This goes on for nearly two hours. The hapless driver gets cramps in both arms, he has rubbed himself raw, has violent knob-ache, his sight is failing (as promised for years by his priest) and despite the cold wind, has collapsed in a sweating, gibbering heap on the ground, unable to stand.

"Do it again," says the Scouser.

"I can't do it anymore – you'll just have to kill me," whimpers the man.

The guy looks down at the pathetic soul slumped on the roadside. "All right, la'," he says. "NOW you can give my daughter a lift into town."

Two Manchester businessmen were sitting down for a break in their soon to be new shop. As yet, the store wasn't ready, with only a few shelves set up.

One said to the other, "I bet you that any minute now some idiot is going to walk by, put his face to the window, and ask what we're selling."

No sooner were the words out of his mouth when, sure enough, a curious Scouser, on a visit to see if there actually was civilization in Manchester, walked to the window, had a peek, and asked, "What are you selling here?"

One of the men replied sarcastically, "We're selling arseholes."

Without skipping a beat, the Scouser said, "You're doing well. Only two left."

2

MAN U BASTARDS

What do you call 20 Manchester United Fans skydiving from an aeroplane?
  Diahorrea.

What do you call a Man Utd season ticket holder?
  Scenery.

What do you say to a Manchester United supporter with a good looking bird on his arm?
  "Nice tattoo."

Someone asked me the other day: "What time does Manchester United kick off?"
  "About every ten minutes," I replied.

What do you call a Manchester United fan with half a brain?
  Gifted.

What do you call a Manchester United fan with lots of girlfriends?
  A shepherd.

What's the difference between a Manchester United fan and a trampoline?

You take your shoes off to jump on a trampoline.

I was talking to the Manchester United groundsman and commenting on how green and lush the grass was.

He replied: "It should be with all the shit that plays on it."

How do you kill a Man U ratboy when he's drinking?

Slam the toilet seat on his head.

Why do Manchester United supporters have moustaches?

So they can look like their mothers.

What's black and brown and looks good on a Manchester United fan?

A rottweiler.

What do you call a Man U fan with no arms or legs?

Trustworthy.

What's the difference between a dead dog and a dead Manchester United fan in the road?

Skid marks in front of the dog.

Why do Manchester United fans whistle while sitting on the toilet?

So they know which end to wipe.

There's a rumour going about that if you buy a season ticket at Old Trafford then you get a free space suit. Apparently it's due to the lack of atmosphere.

A man desperate at the ill nature of his life as a Manchester United fan decides to top himself. In his living room, alone, he prepares to hang himself. At the very last moment, he decides upon wearing his full Man U kit as his last statement. A neighbour, catching sight of the impending incident, informs the police. On arrival, the police quickly remove the United kit and dress the man in stockings and sus-penders. The man, totally confused asks why.

The policeman simply replies, "It's to avoid embarrassing your family."

Did you hear about the Man United fan who studied for two weeks for his urine test?

A guy goes to the doctor and says to the doc: "There's summat wrong with my arse."

The doc asks: "What is it?"

The guy says: "It keeps singing 'Glory, glory Man Utd'. "

The doc says: "Don't worry, lots of arseholes sing that."

Why does NASA send its astronauts to train at Old Trafford?

It's the only place in the world with no atmosphere.

A policeman caught a fan climbing the wall at Old Trafford.

He made him go back and watch the rest of the match.

You're trapped in a room with a tiger, a rattlesnake, and a Manchester United fan. You have a gun with two bullets. What should you do?

Shoot the United fan. Twice.

What do you get when you offer a Manchester United fan a penny for his thoughts?

Change.

How many Man U fans does it take to pave up a driveway?

Depends how thin you slice them.

What's the difference between a Man U fan and a vibrator?

A Man U fan is a real dick

How many Man U supporters does it take to stop a moving bus?

Never enough.

What would you call a pregnant Man United fan?

A dope carrier.

What do you get if you see a Manchester United fan buried up to his neck in sand?

More sand.

A Leeds fan, an Arsenal fan and a Manchester United fan escape from prison. They ran for miles until they came upon an old barn where they decided to hide in the hayloft and rest. When they climbed up, they found three large sacks and decided to climb into them for camouflage.

About an hour later two police officers came into the barn. The sergeant told the constable to go up and check out the hayloft. When he got up there the sergeant asked him what he saw and the constable yelled back, "Just three sacks."

The sergeant told him to find out what was in them, so the constable kicked the first sack, which

had the Leeds fan in it. He went: "Woof", so the constable told the sergeant there was a dog in it.

Then he kicked the sack with the Arsenal fan in it. He went: "Meow", so he told him there was a cat in it.

Then he kicked the one with the scum fan in it, and there was no sound at all. So he kicked it six more times, and finally the scum fan said: "Potatoes".

Top tip for Manchester United fans: don't waste money on expensive new kits every season. Simply strap a large inflatable penis to your forehead, and everyone will immediately know which team you support.

Name three football clubs that contain swear words?

Arsenal, Scunthorpe and Man fucking Utd.

Michael Barrymore has offered Manchester United a million pounds to play as their striker because he wants 10 pricks behind him and 67,000 assholes jumping up and down.

EUROPEAN CUP THOUGHTS:

NEWS FLASH
Swine flu update:
30,000 Mancs in Italy
Pig sick

For all those Manchester United fans out there who are clinically depressed about the result of that game. Today a special helpline has been set up by Sir Alex Ferguson: Simply call 0800 10 10 10.

Calls charged at peak rate for overseas users.

Once again the number is 0800 won nothing won nothing won nothing.

I've just heard the terrible news that Lionel Messi's house was broken into during the European Cup game.

Police have made a statement that they would like to question the Man Utd midfield, as they were nowhere to be seen between the hours of 19.45 and 22.00.

FOR SALE: 30,000 Man U flags – only waved for ten minutes

Man U fans are being investigated as part of the expenses scandal.

Apparently 90 percent of them have been claiming for a second home in Manchester.

After the Champions League Final North West Water had to issue a flash flood warning, due to millions of Scousers pissing themselves laughing.

What have Man U and a nappy got in common?

Piss up front and crap at the back.

What shall we do with the Man U bastards?
What shall we do with the Man U bastards?
What shall we do with the Man U bastards?
Early in the morning?

Shoot, shoot, shoot the bastards
Shoot, shoot, shoot the bastards
Shoot, shoot, shoot the bastards

Early in the morning.

A Scouser meets a friend and sees that his friend's car is a total write-off, covered in leaves, grass, branches, dirt and blood. He asks his friend: "What's happened to your car?"

"Well," the friend replies, "I ran over Rio Ferdinand."

"OK," says the man, "that explains the blood, but what about the leaves, the grass, the branches and the dirt?"

"Well, he tried to escape through the park."

3

FAIRY TALES

A golfer playing in Ireland hooked his drive into the woods. Looking for his ball, he found a little leprechaun flat on his back, a big bump on his head and the golfer's ball beside him.

Horrified, the golfer got his water bottle from the cart and poured it over the little guy, reviving him.

"Arrgh! What happened?" the leprechaun asked.

"I'm afraid I hit you with my golf ball," the golfer says.

"Oh, I see. Well, ye got me fair and square. Ye get three wishes, so what do you want?"

"Thank God, you're all right!" the golfer answers in relief. "I don't want anything, I'm just glad you're OK, and I apologize."

And the golfer walks off. "What a nice guy," the leprechaun says to himself. "I have to do something for him. I'll give him the three things I would want: a great golf style, all the money he ever needs, and a fantastic sex life."

A year goes by (as it does in stories like this) and the golfer is back. On the same hole, he again hits a

bad drive into the woods and the leprechaun is there waiting for him.

"Twas me that made ye hit the ball here," the little guy says. "I just want to ask ye, how's yer game?"

"My game is fantastic." the golfer answers. "I'm an internationally famous amateur golfer now." He adds, "By the way, it's good to see that you're all right."

"Oh, I'm fine now, thank ye. I did that for yer golf game, you know. And tell me, how's yer money situation?"

"Why, it's just wonderful!" the golfer states. "When I need cash, I just reach into my pocket and pull out money I didn't even know was there."

"I did that fer ye also." And tell me, how's yer sex life?" The golfer blushes, turns his head away in embarrassment, and says shyly, "It's OK."

"Ah c'mon now," urged the leprechaun, "I'm wanting to know if I did a good job. How many times a week?"

Blushing even more, the golfer looks around then whispers, "Once, sometimes twice a week."

"What?" responds the Leprechaun in shock. "That's all? Only once or twice a week?"

"Well," says the golfer, "that's not bad for a Catholic priest in Speke."

A married couple in their early 60s were celebrating their 35th wedding anniversary in a quiet, romantic little restaurant.

Suddenly, a tiny beautiful fairy appeared on their table saying, "For being such an exemplary married couple and for being loving to each other for all this time, I will grant you each a wish."

"Oh, I want to travel around the world with my darling husband," said the woman.

The fairy waved her magic wand and poof (it's a Manchester fairy) two tickets for a cruise appeared in her hands.

The husband thought for a moment. "Well, this is all very romantic, but an opportunity like this will never come again. I'm sorry my love, but my wish is to have a wife 30 years younger than me."

The wife and the fairy were deeply disappointed, but a wish is a wish. So the fairy waved her magic wand and poof!

The husband became 92 years old.

The moral of this story:

Men who are ungrateful bastards should remember, fairies are female.

Except of course in some parts of Manchester.

4

SCOUSER HUMOUR

There is a new study just released by the Psychiatric Association about Liverpool women and how they feel about their arses. The results are pretty interesting.

1. Five percent of women surveyed feel their arse is too big.

2. Ten percent of women surveyed feel their arse is too small.

3. The remaining 85 percent say they don't care; they love him; he's a good man, and they would have married him anyway.

In Speke, a policeman was making his evening rounds. As he was checking a second hand car sales lot, he came upon two wee old biddies sitting in a car. He stopped and asked them why they were sitting there in the car.

Were they trying to steal it?

"No, no, son, we bought it."

"Then why don't you drive it away."

"We can't drive."

"Then why did you buy it?"

"We were told that if we bought a used car here we'd get fucked. So we're just waiting."

Mick the Scouser wants a job as a signalman on the railways. He is told to meet Inspector Johnston at the signal box. The inspector puts this question to him: "What would you do if you realised that two trains were heading for each other on the same track?"

Says Mick: "I would switch the points for one of the trains."

"What if the lever broke?" asked the Inspector.

"Then I'd dash down out of the signal box," said Mick, "and I'd use the manual lever over there."

"What if that had been struck by lightning?"

"Then," Mick continues, "I'd run back into the signal box and phone the next signal box."

"What if the phone was engaged?"

"Next," persevered Mick, "I'd rush down out of the box and use the public emergency phone at the level crossing up there."

"What if that was vandalised?"

"Oh well, then I'd run and get my Uncle Sean."

This puzzled the Inspector, so he asked, "Why on earth would you do that?"

Mick replied: "Because he's never seen a train crash."

Mick of course got the job, and was found one day with one half of the manually operated level crossing gate open and the other half closed.

When the signalman was asked why, he replied: "Well, I'm half expecting a train."

At the wake held for a notorious scally robber and fighter, a sudden silence fell. To break it, someone said:

"Who can say something good about young Phil?"

The silence deepened. Then at last one of the mourners spoke:

"His brother was worse."

Last night my wife and I were sitting in our kitchen in Speke and I said to her, "I never want to live in a vegetative state, dependent on some machine and fluids from a bottle to keep me alive. That would be no quality of life at all. If that ever happens, just pull the plug."

So she got up, unplugged the computer, and threw out my whisky.

Manc Bitch.

A first year Liverpool Uni student had just got an old banger as a starting present from his parents. He took it for a spin but misjudged the road and over-turned the car directly between the house of Mr. and Mrs. Smith and Mr. and Mrs. Balls.

Luckily, he was pulled out by the Smiths.

Bobby and Davy from Anfield are Siamese twins, who go to France. An on-duty gendarme spots their hired car approaching the Champs Elysees with a rear light broken. He beckons the driver to pull over, which he does and winds his window down.

The officer has a good look inside the car and notices that the driver and passenger are conjoined twins. Instead of making an issue over the light out situation he begins to engage in some friendly chat.

Gendarme. "Ah, you are on holiday my friends?"

Davy. "That's right. We've been coming every September for the last nine years."

Gendarme. "So you come to France to get away from ze rainy weather you have in England?"

Davy. "Na, it nearly always pisses down when we come here. Your weather's no better than ours, isn't that right Bobby?"

Bobby. "Aye."

Gendarme. "Zen I take it you are here to enjoy our delicious French food – very healthy."

Davy. "Na, yer food's rotten, everything reeks of garlic. We've brought a box full of sarnies to avoid eating your crap."

Gendarme. "Zen you must be here to drink our famous wines and cognac, surely."

Davy. "Yer booze is crap as well. We've had to bring a carry in. Isn't that right Bobby?"

Bobby. "Aye."

Gendarme (by now ever so slightly bemused). "Well in that case you must be here to see the Parisienne madamoiselles, ze most beautiful women in Europe."

Davy. "Yer kiddin? The berds here are dogs, I wouldn't touch them with yours."

Gendarme (by now rather irate). "Zen why do you people come to our country if everysing ees so bad?"

Bobby. "It's the only chance our Dave gets to drive!"

5

MANC AND SCOUSER POETRY

'Twas an evening in November,
As I very well remember.
I was strolling down the street in drunken pride,
But my knees were all aflutter,
So I landed in the gutter,
And a pig came up and laid down by my side.
Yes, I lay there in the gutter,
Thinking thoughts I could not utter,
When a lady passing by did softly say,
"You can tell a man that boozes
By the company he chooses."
And the pig got up and slowly walked away.

Female Scouser's Prayer.

Dear Lord,
I pray for Wisdom to understand my man;
Love to forgive him;
And Patience for his moods;
Because Lord, if I pray for Strength,
I'll beat the bastard to death.

6

MANCS AND LIGHT BULBS

Q. How many Manchester United fans does it take to change a light bulb?

A. (I) Three. One to change the light bulb, one to buy the "2010 light bulb changing" commemorative t-shirt and video, and one to drive the other two back to Torquay.

(II) Who cares, so long as it comes out in 4 different versions (£49.99 each), and changes twice every season?

How many people does it take to change a light bulb at Old Trafford?

One person to change the light bulb, one person to tap irritatingly on a watch whilst chewing gum like a madman, several thousand people to watch in silence and several million people to bang on about how well the light bulb was changed and how no one else could do it as well as "their person" did despite not seeing the light bulb being changed.

How does Rio Ferdinand change a lightbulb?

He holds it in the air, and the world revolves around him.

How many Man United fans does it take to change a light bulb?

560,001. That is one to change it, 60,000 to say they've been changing it for years and 500,000 to buy the replica kit.

7

EXAMS FOR MANCS

Maths made easy with Manchester United:

From The Official MUFC Maths Workbook, which covers sums for practising Key Stage Two maths for 7–11-year-olds. This has been introduced as part of the Government's maths campaign.

1. Rio is 78 yards away from the referee at Old Trafford and Wayne is 65 yards away. If Rio can run at 21mph and Wayne can run at 16mph, who will be sticking their vein-bulging forehead into the hapless whistler's face first, assuming Rio does not stop to stamp on an opponent on his way.

2. If one minute of time is taken up in a game for substitutions and one minute for injuries, how much injury time will be added on by the referee if Man Utd are losing at home?

3. Ryan is a Welshman. Express, as a percentage, the number of internationals he has missed on a Wednesday evening compared to the miraculous recoveries he made for the following Saturday.

4. Manchester United are one of the giants of world club football. How many more European Cup Finals have they appeared in than Steaua Bucharest? (For one extra mark: How many more than Reims?)

4a. How many more times have Manchester United won the European Cup than Nottingham Forest?

5. Phil Neville had 30 international caps while he played for Man U. If you take away the number of appearances when he was the only adult male in England who could just about kick the ball with his left foot, how many are left?

6. You are the referee at Old Trafford. How near to a visiting defender does a tumbling Owen have to be to earn a penalty if he goes down in the box? (Note: Round your answers down to the nearest 20 yards.)

6a. Probability. Express the statistical probability of visitors to Old Trafford being awarded a penalty. Compare this with the probability of opponents of Manchester United being awarded a penalty home or away, and then discuss if a penalty awarded to Manchester United would be awarded to their opponents in identical circumstances.

7. Mark "The Red" lives in Guildford. How much does it cost for him and his two sons to travel to the Theatre of Silence every other weekend, including limited edition matchday programme, a few drinks and prawn sandwiches all round? How much could he save per week if he watched his local team instead? (Note: Round your answers down to the nearest thousand pounds).

8. Berbatov is very cunning and fast. How much pressure need be applied to make him tumble over in the opponents' penalty area? (Note: Answers must be in lbs per square inch. However, answers such as, 'However much pressure is applied by Ferguson to referees' are accepted.)

9. Alex has won it once, Bob has won it four times. Alex has one, Bob does not. What am I talking about? Explain your answer (because nobody else can).

Exam to Become a Manc:

PART I (WRITTEN)

INSTRUCTIONS TO CANDIDATES

(a) Do not attempt to answer more than one question at a time.

(b) Do not attempt to write on both sides of the paper at the same time.

(c) On no account attempt Question 3.

(d) Slide rules O.K.

N.B. Candidates caught cheating will be given extra marks for initiative. All candidates are requested to use separate answer books.

Time Allowed: six weeks

1. Who won the Second World War? Who came second?

2. Explain in one sentence Einstein's Theory of Relativity OR write your name in block capitals.

3. What is the number of this question?

4. Name the odd man out: The Chief Rabbi, The Pope, Jack the Ripper, The Archbishop of Canterbury.

5. At the All-England Sheepdog Trials of 2009, how many sheepdogs were found guilty?

6. At what time is the nine o'clock news broadcast?

7. Spell each of the following words: DOG, CAT, PIG.

8. Write a tongue twister three times quickly.

9. There have been six kings of England named George. The latest was George the Sixth – name the other five.

10. Quote four lines from any poem written in the English language or from any other poem written in the English language.

N.B. This is the honours paper – there is a special pass version for Cockneys.

PART II (PRACTICAL)

Leave the examination hall and persuade the first passer-by you meet to accompany you through life, using irony where necessary.

8

PARTY TIME

Jack the Manc has been in the computer business for 25 years and is sick of the stress. An auntie dies and leaves him a little flat in Dingle, so he takes a deep breath and moves there to write a book. He only ever sees the postman and gets his groceries once a month. After six months or so of almost total isolation, he's finishing a meal when someone knocks on his door. He opens it and there is a huge ragged-arsed Scouser in trackies standing there.

"Name's Jimmy. I'm your neighbour from downstairs. I am having a party on Saturday. Thought you might like to come."

"Great," says Jack, "after six months of this I'm ready to meet some local folk. Thank you."

As Jimmy is leaving he stops, "I should warn you there is likely to be some drinking."

"Not a problem. After 25 years in the computer business, I can drink with the best of them."

Again, as he starts to leave Jimmy stops. "More than likely there will be some fierce fighting too."

"Well, I get on with most people, and if I don't, I can handle myself. I'll be there. Thanks again."

Once again Jimmy turns from the door. "I've seen some wild sex at these parties, too."

"Now that's not a problem" says Jack, "Remember I've been on my own for six months. I'll definitely be there. By the way, what should I wear?"

Jimmy stops in the doorway again and says, "Whatever you want, it will just be the two of us."

A Scouse woman and a man from Manchester were stranded on a desert island after a shipwreck. Their clothes were in rags and their food running out.

"I suppose it could always be worse," said the woman.

"Oh, yes, it could," agreed the Manc. "I might have bought a return ticket."

One day, after winning ten grand at the races a Mancunian walked into a bar in downtown Liverpool.

"I'm lookin' for the roughest and toughest whore in Liverpool!" he roared to the barman.

"We've got her!" replied the barman. "She's upstairs in the second room on the right."

The Manc handed the bartender a £50 note to pay for the whore and two bottles of beer.

He grabbed the bottles, stamped up the stairs, kicked open the second door on the right and yelled, "I'm lookin' for the roughest and toughest whore in Liverpool!"

The woman inside the room looked at the Manc and said, "You found her!"

Then she stripped naked, bent over and grabbed her ankles.

"How do you know I want to do it in that position?" asked the man.

"I don't," replied the whore, "I just thought you might like to open those bottles first."

"Why don't you give up the drinking, smoking and carousing?" said the do-gooding Manc visitor.

"It's too late," replied Scouse John.

"It's never too late," assured the virtuous one.

"Well, there's no rush then," smiled John.

9

MAN U WIT AND WISDOM

Alex the Ferg is visiting the Emirates. Arsene Wenger tells him that foreign footballers are more intelligent than home grown.

"I don't think so," says Alex. Arsene calls Cesc Fabregas over. "Your father's son is not your brother. Who is he?"

"That's easy," says Cesc. "It's me."

Next day Alex calls Wayne in. "Tell me son, your father's son is not your brother. Who is he?"

Rooney thinks and says: "Can I think about it boss, and come back to you?"

That night he asks Coleen the same question.

"I'm not sure" she says, "phone Fletcher. He'll know."

Wayne phones and asks. Fletcher says: "That's easy. It's me."

Next day Wayne goes to see the boss: "I've worked it out. It's Darren Fletcher."

"Get off, ye daft bugger," says Alex, "It's Cesc Fabregas."

Rooney, Rioscum and Ferguson are all trapped on the roof of a burning building in Liverpool, obviously started by accident, M'lud.

The Fire Brigade duly arrive and hold out the big blanket for the guys to jump onto. They are understandably all a bit nervous, but, being a brave lad and the club captain, Rioscum goes first. At the last second, the firemen whip the blanket away and Rioscum splats on the pavement, dead.

Still giggling, the firemen shout to Ferguson to go next. He jumps, they move the blanket, he makes a pancake on the pavement, high fives all round from the firemen.

Last to go is Rooney. But he's not having any of it.

"You'll move the blanket!" he shouts.

"No we won't," they reply.

"It's no good, I don't trust you. You'll move the blanket again!" shouts the traitor.

"Come on, jump you fool!" they shout.

"Well, alri'," he replies. "But I'm not jumping until you put the blanket down and move at least ten yards away from it."

What's the difference between listening to Alex Ferguson's after-match interview and childbirth?

One's an extremely painful, almost unbearable experience, and the other one's just having a baby.

Rooney, Giggs and Ferdinand were training on a Wednesday afternoon when Ferdinand says: "Why don't we skive off? The boss leaves at noon on Wednesdays and never calls or rings or nowt, he'd never know."

They all skived off. Ferdinand went to the pictures, Giggs went to the zoo (like the good Welsh lad he is) and Rooney thought he would surprise his missus. He arrived home and spied through the window to see his boss wedged firmly up Coleen.

Next Wednesday afternoon, Ferdinand suggested they skive off again, Giggs agreed but Rooney said: "No fear, I nearly got caught last week."

Tributes have been pouring in over the sad news of the death of Sir Stanley Matthews last Wednesday:

Kevin Keegan said he was "a legend".

George Best described his talent as "sublime".

Bobby Charlton called him "a Brazilian in an England shirt".

Gary Lineker was quoted as saying, "He was the last great gentleman of the game."

Wayne Rooney said, "It's a real shame. Coleen and I loved his Turkey Drummers. They're bootiful."

There's a fiery crash involving a limousine not far from Old Trafford. The passengers are burned almost beyond recognition, but it's believed that Fletcher was one of them. So the coroner calls his mates Ferdinand and Rooney to identify the body. Neither can tell by looking at the face, so Ferdinand says, "Roll him over."

"Yeh, roll him over," says Rooney, "Then we'll be able to tell if it's him."

"How will that help?" asks the coroner.

"If there's two arseholes, it's him," replies Rio.

"Two arseholes? How do you know he had two arseholes?" asks the coroner.

"Everybody knows that," says Rooney. "Every time the three of us showed up at the ground together somebody was sure to say: 'Here comes that Fletcher with those two arseholes'."

"He's said to me half a dozen times, 'I played centre-half for the school you know.' I said: 'Yes, but not against Didier Drogba.'"

Sir Alex tries to curb Wayne Rooney's enthusiasm.

"Thanks for giving me the best night of my life – but please don't tell my wife!"

Berbatov reveals the sentence he hears most when leaving.

A Prediction: Spurs 1 Manchester United 8

Manchester United's march towards the 2010 Premiership title continued today with a stunning display at White Hart Lane. The Super Reds went ahead just before the kick-off when Giggs was sent away down the left wing.

His cross was handled on the halfway line by a Spurs defender and a penalty was awarded for this cynical foul. Berbatov stepped up to slot the ball home for United's 33rd penalty of the season. It was no more than United deserved.

The 15th minute saw the Super-Smashing Reds go two up after Michael Dawson was penalised for coughing just outside the area. Rooney's resultant free kick was slightly miss-hit, but even if the keeper was not being pinned to the floor by Rio Ferdinad, he would not have saved it. 2–0. It was no more than United deserved.

The 21st minute saw more trouble for Spurs when Jermain Defoe was sent off for enquiring about the referee's Man United shirt. However, two minutes after the interval, Spurs struck back after an amazing piece of good fortune. The referee's assistant could only parry Darren Bent's shot and Robbie Keane thumped the ball home. Confusion reigned for 10 minutes as the entire Manchester

United squad surrounded the referee, arguing that the referee's assistant had been fouled 15 minutes earlier. The referee grudgingly had to give the goal even though he racked his brain for a reason to disallow it.

Alex Ferguson was furious and rushed down from his seat in the stand to the dugout, knocking over a number of blind, disabled, pensioners in wheelchairs on the way down. Fortunately, things settled down again as Paul Scholes took a long-range shot, which deflected off the corner flag but had clearly crossed the line, 3–1. It was no more than United deserved.

Just after the restart, un-sportsmanlike Ledley King was dismissed for making ridiculous claims for a penalty after Vidic had nearly decapitated Robbie Keane. The referee and his assistant missed the incident as they were both asking Rio for his autograph, but replays showed that Vidic's flying kung-fu kick, followed by a forearm smash was clearly unintentional.

Ten minutes later Ferguson took off Scholes and replaced him with Foster, Park and Tosic. Wonderful, wonderful Man United's fourth came shortly after. Robbie Keane was caught offside just outside the Spurs penalty area and the Giggs free-kick thundered in after deflecting off the underside

of the floodlights. It was no more than United deserved.

The super, marvel, wonder Reds kept the pressure on until the bitter end. In the 98th minute Alan Hutton conceded a free kick just outside his own area for blatantly glancing at the referee. Giggs stepped up and proceeded to chip the ball right into the referee's path and he made no mistake from 10 yards. Goal number five and it was no more than United deserved.

Berbatov slotted home number six from the penalty spot after Roman Pavlyuchenko went down with a broken leg. Fortunately Ferdinand was nearby when it happened and, after running 50 yards, he was able to bring the incident to the referee's attention. Unfazed by Pavlyuchenko's cynical tactics, protruding bone and spraying blood, the referee sent him off for diving (and time wasting) and awarded United the penalty. Berbatov cheekily chipped the ball over the keeper and the crossbar, but the referee decided that it was a goal, because based on past records, Berbatov rarely missed.

When the final whistle went after 33 minutes of injury time, Spurs traipsed off with their heads low, having been taught a footballing lesson by what is by far the greatest team the world has ever seen. As the losers hit the showers, a superb flowing movement

by United culminated with a fine diving header by Alex Ferguson and it was 7–1. However the referee decided that it was such a good goal, it should count double.

8–1 then – and it was no more than United deserved.

10

SCOUSER ENTERPRISE

Ah, Scousers and enterprise. A scally in Anfield has had one of those blue plaques put up outside his door and is receiving a steady stream of visitors. It reads: "Once the youngest person in the world."

A Scouser and a Manc were standing on a corner arguing, as they do, when a Londoner approached them.

"You know," said the Londoner, "I just went into that pub over there, ordered a pint, played some darts and when I walked out of the pub the barman said to me: 'Pay up.' I told him I paid when I got my pint, the barman did nothing, so I got a free drink."

The Manc was intrigued with the idea so much he went into the pub and did the same thing the Londoner did. The Manc came out and told the Londoner and the Scouser that the barman gave him no trouble either.

So the Scouser gives it a try. He walks into the bar and orders a pint. As he talks with the barman, the barman mentioned the two blokes who walked out

without paying. The Scouser asked the barman why he did nothing. The barman said: "I don't need any trouble."

The Scouser replied: "Well, it's getting late. If you give me my change, I'll be heading home."

A Texan saunters into a pub in Liverpool and clears his voice to the crowd of drinkers. He announces, "I hear you Scouse guys are a bunch of hard drinkers. I'll give 500 American dollars to anybody in here who can drink 10 pints of Guinness back-to-back." The room goes very quiet and no one dares to take up the Texan's offer. One local even leaves.

Thirty minutes later the guy who left returns and taps the Texan on the shoulder. "Is your offer still good?" inquires the Scouser. The Texan says yes and asks the bartender to line up ten pints of Guinness. Immediately the Scouser tears into all ten of the pint glasses drinking them back-to-back. The other pub patrons cheer wildly as the Texan sits astonished. The Texan gives the man the $500 and says, "If ya don't mind me askin', just where did you go for half an hour?"

The scally replied, "Oh, I had to trip down to the other pub to see if I could do it."

Four men were being interviewed for a job.

The interviewer asked No 1, "What is the fastest thing you know of?"

The first man replied, "A thought. It pops into your head, there's no forewarning that it's on the way; it's just there. A thought is the fastest thing I know of."

"That's very good," replied the interviewer.

"And now you," he asked No 2.

"Hmmm, let me see . . . a blink!" said the second man. "It comes and goes and you don't know it ever happened. A blink is the fastest thing I know of."

"Excellent!" said the interviewer. "The blink of an eye. That's a very popular cliché for speed."

He then turned to No 3 who was contemplating his reply.

"Well, you step into my house and on the wall there is a light switch. When you flick that switch the light comes on in an instant. Turning on a light is the fastest thing I can think of."

The interviewer was very impressed with the third answer and thought he had found his man. "It's hard to beat the speed of light," he said.

Turning to the fourth man, a Scouser, he posed the same question.

"After hearing the three previous answers, it's

obvious to me the fastest thing known is diarrhoea," said the man.

"What?" said the interviewer, stunned by the response.

"Oh, I can explain," said the guy. "You see, the other day I wasn't feeling too well and ran for the bathroom. But, before I could think, blink, or turn on the light, I shit myself."

11

MAN U AND GOD

Wayne Rooney, Darren Fletcher and Alex Ferguson are standing before God at the Throne of Heaven.

God looks at them and says, "Before granting you a place at my side, I must first ask you what you believe in."

Addressing Rooney first he asks, "What do you believe?"

Wayne looks God in the eye and states passionately, "I believe football to be the food of life. Nothing else brings such unbridled joy to so many people from the slums of Rio to the bright lights of Barcelona. I have devoted my life to bring such joy to people who sat and stood on the terraces supporting their club."

God looks up and offers Wayne the seat to his left.

He then turns to Fletcher, "And you, Darren, what do you believe?"

Darren stands tall and proud, "I believe courage, honour and passion are the fundamentals of life and

I've spent my whole playing career providing a living embodiment of these traits."

God, moved by the passion of the speech offers Darren the seat to his right.

Finally, he turns to Ferguson, "And you, Sir Alex, what do you believe?"

"I believe," says Sir Alex, "that you're sitting in my seat."

A little boy from Liverpool had gone to Rome on holiday with his family hoping to see the Pope. A couple of days after they'd arrived the Pope was doing a tour of the city in his Popemobile.

The little lad was a bit worried that the Pope wouldn't be able to pick him out in the crowd, so his Mum said: "Don't worry, the Pope is a footy fan, so wear your Liverpool shirt and he's bound to pick you out and talk to you."

They're in the crowd, but the Popemobile drives past them, and stops a bit further down the street where John Paul gets out and speaks to a little boy in a Man U shirt. The Liverpool lad is distraught and starts crying.

His Mum says: "Don't worry, the Pope's driving around tomorrow as well, so we'll get you a Man Utd shirt and then he's bound to stop to see you."

The next day arrives, and the boy's got on his new

Man Utd shirt. The Popemobile stops right by him, Il Papa gets out, bends down and says to the lad: "I thought I told you fuck off yesterday."

A Scouse van driver used to amuse himself by running over every Manchester United fan he would see strutting down the side of the road in their ubiquitous red colours. He would swerve to hit them and there would be a loud "Thump!" and then he would swerve back on the road. One day, as the driver was driving along, he saw a priest hitchhiking. He thought he would do a good turn and pulled the van over.

He asked the priest, "Where are you going, Father?"

"I'm going to say mass at St. Joseph's, about two miles down the road," replied the priest.

"No problem, Father. I'll give you a lift. Climb in."

The happy priest climbed into the passenger seat and the van continued down the road. Suddenly the driver saw a Manchester United fan walking down the road and instinctively swerved to hit him. But, just in time, he remembered the priest, so at the last minute he swerved back to the road, narrowly missing the scum bastard. However, even though he was certain he missed the glory-hunting shite, he still heard a loud "Thud!"

Not understanding where the noise came from, he glanced in his mirrors and when he didn't see anything he turned to the priest and said, "I'm sorry, Father, I almost hit that Manchester United fan."

"That's okay," replied the priest. "I got the fucker with the door!"

12

AGE DOES NOT COME ALONE

Liverpudlians have much shorter life spans than do Mancunians and Manchester is said to have one of the lowest mortality rates in the country, the reason being that most people wouldn't be found dead there. Large parts of Liverpool, you know the ones, are getting to look like outdoor retirement homes. Here are a few tips that will tell you how to recognize how much you have aged.

The park has a bench with your name on it already.

Your doctor doesn't give you x-rays any more, but just holds you up to the light.

You remember when the Dead Sea was only sick.

You know all the answers, but nobody asks the questions.

When your wife says, "Let's go upstairs and make love," you answer, "I can't do both!"

Going braless pulls all the wrinkles out of your face.

You don't care where your spouse goes, just as long as you don't have to go too.

You and your teeth don't sleep together.

Your back goes out, but you stay in.

You wake up looking like your passport picture.

Your idea of a night out is sitting on the front steps.

Happy hour is a nap.

Your idea of weightlifting is standing up.

It takes longer to rest than it did to get tired.

The twinkle in your eye is only the reflection of the sun on your bifocals.

You sit in a rocking chair and can't get it going.

You wonder how you could be over the hill when you don't even remember being on top of it.

You don't know real embarrassment until your hip sets off a metal detector.

Every time you suck in your belly, your ankles swell.

Age always corresponds inversely to the size of your multivitamin.

It's harder and harder for sexual harassment charges to stick.

Your secrets are safe with your friends because they can't remember them either.

No one expects you to run into a burning building.

There's nothing left to learn the hard way.

Your joints are more accurate than the BBC Weather Service.

You're sitting on a park bench, and a Boy Scout comes up and helps you cross your legs.

Someone compliments you on your layered look, and you're wearing a bikini.

You start videotaping daytime game shows.

Conversations with people your own age often turn into "dueling ailments".

You run out of breath walking DOWN a flight of stairs.

You look both ways before crossing a room.

You frequently find yourself telling people what a loaf USED to cost.

You realize that a stamp today costs more than a movie did when you were growing up.

Many of your co-workers were born the same year that you got your last promotion.

The clothes you've put away until they come back in style come back in style.

The car that you bought brand new becomes an antique.

You're asleep, but others worry that you're dead.

You quit trying to hold your stomach in, no matter who walks into the room.

Your best friend is dating someone half their age and isn't breaking any laws.

Your arms are almost too short to read the Echo.

You enjoy hearing about other people's operations.

You consider coffee one of the most important things in life.

The end of your tie doesn't come anywhere near the top of your trousers.

You know what the word 'equity' means.

Your ears are hairier than your head.

You talk about 'good grass' and you're referring to someone's lawn.

You have a party and the neighbours don't even realize it.

Everything that works hurts, and what doesn't hurt doesn't work.

You feel like the morning after, and you haven't been anywhere.

Your little black book only contains names starting with Dr.

Your knees buckle and your belt won't.

You sink your teeth into a steak, and they stay there.

An old Scouser was boasting to his neighbour, "I've just bought a new hearing aid. It cost me

four thousand pounds, but it's state of the art. It's perfect."

"Really," answered the neighbour. "What kind is it?"

"Half past twelve."

An 80-year-old Liverpudlian goes to the doctor for a check-up. The doctor is amazed at what good shape the guy is in and asks, "How do you stay in such great physical condition?"

"I am a golfer," says the old guy. "I'm up well before daylight and out golfing up and down the fairways. Have a spot of whisky, and all is well."

"Well," says the doctor, "I'm sure that helps, but there's got to be more to it. How old was your Dad when he died?"

"Who said my Dad's dead?"

The doctor is amazed. "You mean you're 80 years old and your Dad's still alive. How old is he?"

"He's 100 years old," says the man. "In fact, he golfed with me this morning, and then we went to the pub for a whisky and for a walk, that's why he's still alive. He's a Scot and he's a golfer, too."

"Well," the doctor says, "That's great, but I'm sure there's more to it than that. How about your Dad's Dad? How old was he when he died?"

"Who said my grandpa's dead?"

Stunned, the doctor asks, "You mean you're 80 years old and your grandfather's still living! Incredible, how old is he?"

"He's 118-years-old," says the guy.

The doctor is getting frustrated at this point. "So, I suppose he went golfing with you this morning, too?"

"No. Grandpa couldn't go this morning because he's getting married today."

At this point the doctor is close to losing it. "Getting married! Why would a 118-year-old guy want to get married?"

"Who said he wanted to?"

The family wheeled Grandma, whose husband, long dead, had made a fortune out of haulage in Liverpool, out on to the lawn, in her wheelchair, where the activities for her 100th birthday were taking place. Grandma couldn't speak very well, but she could write notes when she needed to communicate. After a short time out on the lawn, Grandma started leaning to the right, so some family members, now living in Manchester, all educated by her and her husband's money, and mostly living in expectation of her death, grabbed her, straightened her up, and stuffed pillows on her right.

A short time later, she started leaning off to her left, so again the family grabbed her and stuffed pillows on her left.

Soon she started leaning forward, so the family members again grabbed her, then tied a pillowcase around her waist to hold her up.

A great grandson, now at Liverpool Uni, arrived late, came running up to Grandma and said. "Hi Great Gran, you're looking great, Gran. How are these jackals treating you?"

Grandma took out her little notepad and slowly wrote a note to the boy. "They won't let me fart."

13

UNLUCKY

A Scouser goes up to his friend Richard from Toxteth because he's been interested in dating his supposedly ex-girlfriend Sarah and starts asking him if they're still dating.

So Tim approaches Richard and starts his investigation: "So, Richard, are you still seeing Sarah?"

Richard looks over to Tim and delivered some hard news on him: "No, she bled to death from her gonorrhoea."

Tim looked over at Richard in disbelief, but then he thought he found one error with this little story so he says to Richard: "Richard, I don't think you bleed to death from gonorrhoea."

Richard says: "When you give it to me you do."

While walking through Calderstones Park a man came upon another man hugging a tree with his ear firmly against the tree. Seeing this he inquired. "Just out of curiosity, what are you doing?"

"I'm listening to the music of the tree," the other man replied.

"You're kiddin' me."

"No, would you like to give it a try?"

Understandably curious, the man says, "Well, OK . . ."

So he wrapped his arms around the tree and pressed his ear up against it. With this, the other man whacks a pair of handcuffs on his wrists, took his wallet, phone, and car keys, then stripped him naked and left.

Two hours later another nature lover strolled by, saw this guy handcuffed to the tree stark naked, and asked, "What happened to you?"

He told the guy the whole terrible story about how he got there. When he finished telling his story, the other guy shook his head in sympathy, walked around behind him, kissed him gently behind the ear and said, "This just isn't going be your day, pretty one."

In ancient Anfield (AD 1965), Wise Willie was widely lauded for his wisdom. One day an acquaintance ran up to him excitedly and said, "Wise Willie, do you know what I just heard about one of your students called Shagger McGraw?"

"Wait a moment," Wise Willie replied. "Before you tell me I'd like you to pass a little test. It's called the Triple Filter Test."

"Triple filter?"

"That's right," Wise Willie continued. "Before you talk to me about my student, let's take a moment to filter what you're going to say. The first Filter is Truth. Have you made absolutely sure that what you are about to tell me is true?"

"No," the man said, "actually I just heard about it and . . ."

"All right," said Wise Willie. "So you don't really know if it's true or not. Now let's try the second filter, the Filter of Goodness. Is what you are about to tell me about my student something good?"

"No, on the contrary . . ."

"So," Wise Willie continued, "you want to tell me something bad about him, even though you're not certain it's true?"

The man shrugged, a little embarrassed.

Wise Willie continued, "You may still pass the test though, because there is a third filter – the Filter of Usefulness. Is what you want to tell me about my student going to be useful to me?"

"No, not really . . ."

"Well," concluded Wise Willie, "if what you want to tell me is neither True, nor Good, nor even Useful, why tell it to me at all?"

The man was defeated and ashamed.

This is the reason Wise Willie was a great philosopher and held in such high esteem. It also explains why he never found out that Shagger McGraw was shagging Wise Willie's wife.

A Liverpudlian was out at the dog racing, all but losing his shirt. Then Peter noticed a priest who stepped out onto the track and blessed the forehead of one of the dogs lining up for the fourth race. Lo and behold, that dog, a very long shot, won the race. Before the next race, as the dogs began lining up, Peter watched with interest as the old priest stepped onto the track. Sure enough, as the fifth race dogs came to the start the priest made a blessing on the forehead of one of the dogs.

Peter made a beeline for a bookie and placed a small bet on the dog. Again, even though it was another long shot, the dog the priest had blessed won the race. Peter collected his winnings, and anxiously waited to see which dog the priest would bless for the sixth race. The priest again blessed a dog.

Peter bet a lot on it, and it won. Peter was elated. As the races continued the priest kept blessing long shot dogs, and each one ended up coming in first. By and by, Peter was pulling in some serious money. By the last race, he knew his wildest dreams were going

to come true. He made a quick dash to the Cashline, withdrew all his savings, and awaited the priest's blessing that would tell him which dog to bet on.

True to his pattern, the priest stepped onto the track for the last race and blessed the forehead of an old greyhound that was the longest shot of the day. Peter also observed the priest blessing the eyes, ears, and feet of the old dog.

Peter knew he had a winner and bet every penny he owned on the old dog. He then watched dumb-founded as the dog came in dead last and then died. Peter, in a state of shock, made his way down to the track area where the priest was.

Confronting the old priest he demanded, "Father! What happened? All day long you blessed dogs and they all won. Then in the last race, the dog you blessed lost by a mile. Now, thanks to you I've lost every penny of my savings. All of it."

The priest nodded wisely and with sympathy. "Son," he said, "that's the problem with you Proddies, you can't tell the difference between a simple blessing and the last rites."

14

THE GOOD, THE BAD AND THE UGLY, MANCHESTER STYLE

Good. Your wife is pregnant.
Bad. It's triplets.
Ugly. You had a vasectomy five years ago.

Good. Your wife's not talking to you.
Bad. She wants a divorce.
Ugly. She's a lawyer.

Good. Your son is finally maturing.
Bad. He's involved with the woman next door.
Ugly. So are you.

Good. Your son studies a lot in his room.
Bad. You find several porn movies hidden there.
Ugly. You're in them.

Good. Your hubby and you agree, no more kids.
Bad. You can't find your birth control pills.
Ugly. Your 12-year-old daughter borrowed them.

Good. Your husband understands fashion.
Bad. He's a cross-dresser.
Ugly. He looks better than you.

Good. You give the 'birds and bees' talk to your
daughter.
Bad. She keeps interrupting.
Ugly. With corrections.

Good. Your son is shagging someone new.
Bad. It's another man.
Ugly. He's your best pal.

15

SCOUSERS AND GOD

A girl from a Liverpool-Irish family went to London to work as a secretary and began sending home money and gifts to her parents. After a few years they asked her to come home for a visit, as her father was getting frail and elderly. She pulled up to the family home in a Rolls Royce and stepped out wearing furs and diamonds.

As she walked into the house her father said: "Hmmm – they seem to be paying secretaries awfully well in London."

The girl took his hands and said, "Dad – I've been meaning to tell you something for years but I didn't want to put it in a letter. I can't hide it from you any longer. I've become a prostitute."

Her father gasped, put his hand on his heart and keeled over. The doctor was called but the old man had clearly lost the will to live. He was put to bed and the priest was called.

As the priest began to administer Extreme Unction, with the mother and daughter weeping and wailing, the old man muttered weakly: "I'm a

goner . . . killed by my own daughter. Killed by the shame of what you've become."

"Please forgive me," his daughter sobbed, "I only wanted to have nice things. I wanted to be able to send you money and the only way I could do it was by becoming a prostitute."

Brushing the priest aside, the old man sat bolt upright in bed, smiling.

"Did you say prostitute? I thought you said Protestant."

The Vatican Tribunal was seeking information about a celebrated Speke man who was said to have been very devout. A priest interviewed a contemporary of the holy man. The man testified thus concerning a miracle he had witnessed:

"Holy Willie came along one day as we were all playing pitch and toss. He was praying and singing hymns. Three big fellows playing pitch and toss had great big sores all over their faces and when Holy Willie saw them he was sorry for them. He closed his eyes and prayed, picked up some dirt from the side of the road and spat upon it. He rubbed the dirt and spittle on the faces of the three men." The witness concluded with the statement: "It was a miracle Holy Willie wasn't killed."

Once upon a time in the Kingdom of Heaven, God went missing for six days. Eventually, the Archangel Gabriel found him, resting on the seventh day. He inquired of God, "Where have you been?"

God breathed a deep sigh of satisfaction and proudly pointed downwards through the clouds, "Look Gabriel, look what I've made."

Archangel Gabriel looked puzzled and said, "What is it?"

"It's a planet," replied God, "and I've put Life on it. I'm going to call it Earth and it's going to be a great place of balance."

"Balance?" inquired Gabriel, still confused.

God explained, pointing to different parts of Earth, "For example, North America will be a place of great opportunity and wealth while South America is going to be poor. Over there I've placed a continent of white people and over there is a continent of black people," God continued, pointing to different countries. "This one will be extremely hot and arid while this one will be very cold and covered in ice."

The Archangel, impressed by God's work, then pointed to a small, populated area in the land of Great Britain and said, "What's that?"

"Ah," said God. "That's Merseyside, the most

glorious place on Earth. There's a beautiful river, glorious parks, and buildings, great music and world dominating football teams. The people from Liverpool are going to be modest, intelligent and humorous and they're going to be found traveling the world as explorers. They'll be extremely sociable, hard-working and high-achieving, and they will be known throughout the world as diplomats and carriers of peace."

Gabriel gasped in wonder and admiration but then proclaimed, "What about balance, God? You said there will be balance!"

God replied wisely, "Wait until you see the lazy, arrogant, bastards I'm putting next to them in Manchester."

A young couple from Liverpool wanted to join the church and the priest told them, "We have a special requirement for new member couples. You must abstain from sex for one whole month."

The couple agreed, but after two and a half weeks returned to the church.

When the priest ushered them into his office, the wife was crying and the husband was obviously very depressed.

"You are back so soon. Is there a problem?" the pastor inquired.

"We are terribly ashamed to admit that we did not manage to abstain from sex for the required month," the young man replied sadly.

The priest asked him what happened.

"Well, the first week was difficult . . . However, we managed to abstain through sheer willpower. The second week was terrible, but with the use of prayer, we managed to abstain. However, the third week was unbearable. We tried cold showers, prayer, reading from the bible . . . anything to keep our minds off carnal thoughts. One afternoon my wife reached for a can of paint and dropped it. When she bent over to pick it up, I was overcome with lust and I just had my way with her right then and there. It was lustful, loud, passionate sex. It lasted for over an hour and when we were finished we were both drenched in sweat," admitted the man, shamefacedly.

The priest lowered his head and said sternly, "You understand this means you will not be welcome in our church."

"We know," said the young man, hanging his head. "We're not welcome at B&Q either."

16

SUFFER THE LITTLE CHILDREN

A little Liverpool lad, sent to the naughty step, was overheard praying.

"Lord, if you can't make me a better boy, don't worry about it. I'm having a really good time the way I am."

A little boy from Dingle, who will go far in the world if he lives, was praying as hard as he could.

"Jesus," he prayed, "I really want a pony."

Jumping up and dashing to the window, he saw that the street was empty.

"Jesus," he prayed again, "I really NEED a pony."

Still, no answer to his prayers.

Suddenly the lad stood up, ran into his parent's bedroom, and grabbed the statuette of the Virgin Mary off the mantelpiece.

He wrapped it up in ten layers of paper, using three rolls of tape and a whole ball of string, then stuffed it inside a box at the very bottom of his wardrobe.

"Okay, Jesus," he said, getting down onto his knees again, "If you ever want to see your mother again . . ."

"Da," asked the Liverpool five-year-old, "What makes children delinquent?"

"Shut up, son. Pour yourself another drink and deal."

A Scouse father asked his 10-year-old son if he knew about the birds and the bees.

"I don't want to know," the child said, bursting into tears. "Promise me you won't tell me."

Confused, the father asked what was wrong.

The boy sobbed, "When I was six, I got the 'There's no Easter Bunny. The Americans made it up' speech.

At seven, I got the 'There's no Tooth Fairy' speech.

When I was eight, you give me the 'There's no Santa' speech.

If you're going to tell me that grown-ups don't really shag, I'll have nothing left to live for."

Two small boys, one Scouse and one Manc, get lost in the woods. Darkness comes down and they near a monastery. Upon entering they are asked

their place of birth, telling the head monk their origins. The Manc lad gets the best of treatment, good food, a good bed near the fireplace. The Scouse lad, however, gets a bowl of cold porridge and is told to sleep by the draughty door to keep the cold out of the room. In the morning the head monk asks the boys how it was. "I dreamt I was in heaven, Father," said the Manc boy. "It was just wonderful."

"I dreamt that I was in hell," said the Scouse boy.

"And what was that like?" asked the Abbott.

"Just like this place, you couldn't get near the fire for fucking Mancs."

After the christening of his baby brother in Liverpool St Jude's church, little Jason sobbed all the way home in the back seat of the car. His father asked him three times what was wrong.

Finally, the boy replied, "That priest said he wanted us brought up in a Christian home, and I wanted to stay with you."

A Scouse Sunday school teacher asked her children as they were on the way to church service. "And why is it necessary to be quiet in church?"

One bright little girl replied, "Because people are sleeping."

A Scouse mother was preparing pancakes for her sons, Kevin age five, and Ryan age three.

The boys began to argue over who would get the first pancake. Their mother saw the opportunity for a moral lesson.

"If Jesus were sitting here, He would say, 'Let my brother have the first pancake, I can wait.' "

Kevin turned to his younger brother and said, "Ryan, you be Jesus."

A Scouse wife invited some people to dinner. At the table, she turned to their six-year-old daughter and said, "Would you like to say grace?"

"I wouldn't know what to say," the girl replied. "Just say what you hear Mummy say," the wife answered.

The daughter bowed her head and said, "Jesus, why the fuck did I invite all these people to dinner?"

Years ago, while packing for a trip my (then) three-year-old daughter was having a wonderful time playing on the bed.

At one point she said, "Daddy, look at this," and stuck out two of her fingers.

Trying to keep her entertained, I reached out and stuck her tiny fingers in my mouth and said, "Daddy's going to eat your fingers," pretending to eat them.

I went back to packing, looked up again and my daughter was standing on the bed staring at her fingers with a devastated look on her face.

I asked, "What's wrong, darling?"

She replied, "Where's my bogey?"

A man wearing a Liverpool top was walking down the street in town and he met a small boy with the same strip. They got talking and the man asked his name.

The boy replied, "Six and seven-eighths."

The man asked him why his parents had given him such a strange name, and he replied, "They just picked it out of a hat."

A teacher asks her class, "What was Churchill famous for?"

Little Toxteth Hughie shouts, "He was the last fucking white man in Britain to be called Winston."

The same teacher asked her students to use the word 'fascinate' in a sentence.

Shelley-Rose put up her hand and said, "My family went to my grandpa's farm, and we all saw his pet sheep. It was fascinating."

The teacher said, "That was good, but I wanted you to use the word 'fascinate', not 'fascinating'."

Sally raised her hand. She said, "My family went to see the Art Galleries and I was fascinated."

The teacher said, "Well, that was good Sally, but I wanted you to use the word 'fascinate', not 'fascinated'."

Toxteth Hughie raised his hand.

The teacher hesitated a bit because of previous encounters, but she finally decided there was no way he could damage the word 'fascinate', so she gave him the nod.

Hughie said, "My auntie Gina has a sweater with ten buttons, but her tits are so big she can only fasten eight."

A Manc blonde gets a job as a teacher in Liverpool. She notices a boy in the field standing alone, while all the other kids are running around. She takes pity on him and decides to speak to him.

"You ok?" she says.

"Yer," he says.

"You can go and play with the other children you know," she says.

"It's best I stay here," he says.

"Why?" asks the Manc.

The boy replies, "Because I'm the fucking goalie."

17

PUNNY, PUNNY, PUNNY

Three Scousers are sitting smoking cannabis. After a few spliffs they run out of gear. One of the men stands up and says, "Look, we've got loads more tobacco, I'll just nip into the kitchen and make one of my speciality spliffs."

Off he goes into the kitchen where he takes some cumin, turmeric and a couple of other spices from the spice rack, grinds them up and rolls them into a spliff.

On his return he hands it to one of his smoking partners who lights it and takes a long puff on it. Within seconds he passes out. Ten minutes go by and he's still out cold, so they decide to take him to Liverpool Royal.

On arrival he is wheeled into Emergency. The doctor returns to his friends and asks, "So what was he doing then? Cannabis?"

"Well sort of," replies one of the guys, "But we ran out of gear, so I made a home-made spliff."

"Oh," replies the doctor, "so what did you put in it?"

"Eh, a bit of cumin, some turmeric and a couple of other spices."

The doctor sighs, "Well, that explains it."

"Why, what's wrong with him?" demands one of the men.

The doctor replies, "He's in a korma."

Far away in the tropical waters of the Caribbean, two prawns were swimming around in the sea. One is called Justin and the other is called Christian, best mates despite being a Manc and a Scouser. The prawns were constantly being harassed and threatened by sharks that inhabited the area.

Finally one day Justin said to Christian. "I'm fed up with being a prawn; I wish I was a shark, and then I wouldn't have any worries about being eaten."

A large mysterious cod appeared and said, "Your wish is granted."

Lo and behold, Justin turned into a shark.

Horrified, Christian immediately swam away, afraid of being eaten by his old mate.

Time passed (as it does) and Justin found life as a shark boring and lonely. All his old mates simply swam away whenever he came close to them. Justin didn't realize that his new menacing appearance was the cause of his sad plight.

While swimming alone one day he saw the mysterious cod again and he thought perhaps the mysterious fish could change him back into a prawn.

He approached the cod and begged to be changed back, and, once again lo and behold, he found himself turned back into a prawn. With tears of joy in his tiny little eyes Justin swam back to his friends and bought them all a cocktail.

The punchline does not involve a prawn cocktail. It's much worse.

Looking around the gathering at the reef he realized he couldn't see his old pal. "Where's Christian?" he asked.

"He's at home, still distraught that his best friend changed sides to the enemy and became a shark," came the reply.

Eager to put things right again and end the mutual pain and torture, he set off to Christian's abode. As he opened the coral gate, memories came flooding back.

He banged on the door and shouted, "It's me, Justin, your old friend, come out and see me again."

Christian replied, "No way, my man, you'll eat me. You're now a shark, the enemy, and I'll not be tricked into being your dinner."

Justin cried back "No, I'm not. That was the old me. I've changed. I've found cod. I'm a prawn again, Christian."

Hugh from Speke, a man who loved completely atrocious puns, adored and admired his girlfriend, Lorraine, to whom he was engaged to be married. Wedding plans were well underway and he was looking forward to spending the rest of his life with Lorraine.

However, a beautiful young lady, called Clare-Leigh Maguire, came to work in his shop and they found that they got on together very well. As time went by, Hughie realised that he was in love with Clare-Leigh and that the love was reciprocated.

Being a gentleman, however, he decided that as he had promised to marry Lorraine he would do so and steadily removed himself from his other relationship.

One day, he and Lorraine were walking down by the docks. As they walked, Lorraine slipped, fell into the Mersey and was swept away and drowned.

He stood on the bank for a few minutes feeling very sad before walking away singing happily.

"I can see Clare-Leigh now Lorraine has gone."

Stevie Wonder is playing his first gig in the Empire and the place is absolutely packed to the rafters.

In a bid to break the ice with his new audience he asks if anyone would like him to play a request. A little toothless half-deaf old Anfield man jumps out of his seat in the first row and shouts at the top of his voice: "Play a jazz chord! Play a jazz chord!"

Amazed that this guy knows about his varied career, the blind impresario starts to play an E minor scale and then goes into a difficult jazz melody for about 10 minutes. When he finishes the whole place goes wild.

The old man jumps up again and shouts: "No Stevie! No! Play a jazz chord, play a jazz chord!"

Stevie is a bit peeved by this, but being the professional that he is, dives straight into a jazz improvisation with his band around the B flat minor chord and really tears the place apart. The crowd goes wild with this impromptu show of his technical expertise.

The old man jumps up again. "No! No! Play a jazz chord Stevie, play a jazz chord!"

Stevie is starting to get really annoyed now as the man doesn't seem to appreciate his playing ability.

Stevie shouts to him from the stage, "OK, smartass. You get up here and do it!"

The old guy climbs up on to the stage, takes hold of the microphone and starts to sing.

"A jazz chord, to say, I love you!"

18

RAINY DAY WOMEN

A Liverpool woman was having a daytime shag while her husband was at work. One wet and rainy day she was in bed with her boyfriend when, to her horror, she heard her husband's car outside.

She looked out of the window and yelled to her lover, "Quick, jump out of the window. My husband's home early."

"I can't jump out the window! It's raining out there."

"If my husband catches us in here, he'll kill us both!" she replied. "He's from Toxteth and has a very quick temper plus a shotgun in the car. The rain is the least of your problems!"

So the boyfriend scrambles out of bed, grabs his clothes and jumps out the window. As he began running down the road in the pouring rain, he discovered he had run right into the middle of a charity run, people dressed as all sorts. So he started running alongside the others, thousands of them. Being naked, with his clothes tucked under his arm, he tried to blend in as best he could.

After a little while, a small group of runners, who had been studying him with some curiosity, jogged closer.

"Do you always run in the nude?" one asked.

"Oh yes," he replied, gasping in air. "It feels so wonderfully free."

Another runner moved alongside.

"Do you always run carrying your clothes with you under your arm?"

"Oh, yes," the guy answered breathlessly. "That way I can get dressed at the end of the run and get in the car to go home."

Then a third runner cast his eyes a little lower and queried, "Do you always wear a condom when you run?"

"No. Just when it's raining."

Paddy met Mick in the Dingle street and said, "Paddy, could you draw your bedroom curtains before making love to your wife in future?"

"Why?" Paddy asked.

"Because," said Mick, "The whole street was laughing when they saw you making love yesterday."

Mick said, "Silly bastards, the laugh's on them. I wasn't at home yesterday."

Two Toxteth blondes, Tracy and Sharon, are talking about their boyfriends.

Tracy says, "I love my boyfriend so much, but he has terrible dandruff and doesn't know what to do about it."

Sharon says, "Give him Head and Shoulders."

Tracy asks, "How do you give shoulders?"

A Liverpool hubby walks into Ann Summers to purchase some see-through lingerie for his Manc wife. He is shown several possibilities that range from £50 to £150 in price, the more see-through, the higher the price. He opts for the sheerest item, pays the £150 and takes the lingerie home.

He presents it to his wife and asks her to go upstairs, put it on and model it for him. Upstairs, the wife thinks, "I have an idea. It's so see-through that it might as well be nothing. I'll not put it on, do the modelling naked and return it tomorrow and get a £150 refund for myself."

So she appears naked at the top of the stairs and strikes a pose.

The husband says, "Jesus! It wasn't that creased in the shop."

Joe the gangster got himself killed. His will provided £30,000 for an elaborate funeral. As the last guests

departed, his Scouse wife Helen turned to her oldest friend.

"Well, I'm sure Joe would be pleased," she said.

"I'm sure you're right," replied Jody, who lowered her voice and leaned in close.

"How much did this really cost?"

"All of it," said Helen, "30,000."

"No!" Jody exclaimed. "I mean, it was very nice, but £30,000?"

Helen answered, "The funeral was £6,500. I donated £500 to the church. The wake, food and drink were another £500. The rest went for the stone."

Jody computed quickly. "£22,500 for a memorial stone? Jesus, how big is it?"

"Two and a half carats."

19

WERDZ

Liverpudlians, bored with the paucity of the words available in the English language, have taken to inventing their own. Here are a few examples.

PICASSO BUM.
A woman whose knickers are too small for her, so that she looks as if she has four buttocks.

TESTICULATING.
Waving your arms around and talking total bollocks.

BLAMESTORMING.
Sitting round in a group, discussing why a deadline was missed or a project failed, and why Rafa Benitez was responsible

SEAGULL MANAGER.
A manager who flies in, makes a lot of noise, shits on everything and everybody, and then leaves.

ARSEMOSIS.
The process by which people seem to absorb success
and advancement by crawling up the arse of the boss
rather than by working hard.

SALMON DAY.
The experience of spending an entire day swimming
upstream only to get fucked and die.

SITCOMs.
Single Income, Two Children, Oppressive Mortgage.
What yuppies turn into when they have children
and one of them stops working to stay home with
the kids or start a 'home business'.

SINBAD.
Single income, no boyfriend and desperate.

AEROPLANE BLONDE.
One who has dyed her hair but still has a 'black box'.

PERCUSSIVE MAINTENANCE.
The fine art of battering the shit out of an
electronic device to get it to work again.

ADMINISPHERE.
The rarefied organisational layers beginning just
above the rank and file. Decisions that fall from the

'adminisphere' are often profoundly inappropriate or irrelevant to the problems they were designed to solve. This is often affiliated with the dreaded 'administrivia' – needless paperwork and processes.

OH NO SECOND.
That minuscule fraction of time in which you realize that you've just made a BIG mistake (e.g. you've hit 'reply all').

GREYHOUND.
A very short skirt, only an inch from the hare.

JIMMY-NO-STARS.
A young man of substandard intelligence; the typical adolescent who works in a burger bar. The 'no-stars' comes from the badges displaying stars that staff at these restaurants wear to show their level of training.

MILLENNIUM DOMES.
The contents of a push-up bra, i.e. extremely impressive when viewed from the outside, but there's actually nothing in there worth seeing.

MONKEY BATH.
A bath so hot, that when lowering yourself in, you go: "Oo! Oo! Oo! Aa! Aa! Aa!"

MYSTERY BUS.
The bus that arrives at the pub on Friday night while you're in the toilet after your 10th pint, and whisks away all the unattractive people, so the place is suddenly packed with stunners when you come back in.

MYSTERY TAXI.
The taxi that arrives at your place on Saturday morning before you wake up, whisks away the stunner you slept with, and leaves a 10-pinter in your bed instead.

BEER JACKET.
The invisible but warm jacket worn when walking home after a booze cruise in January. At 3 am.

BEER COMPASS.
The invisible device that ensures your safe arrival home after the booze cruise, even though you're too drunk to remember where you live, how you got here, and where you've come from.

BREAKING THE SEAL.
Your first pee in the pub, usually after two hours of drinking. After breaking the seal of your bladder, repeat visits to the toilet will be required every 10 or 15 minutes for the rest of the night.

TART FUEL.
Bottled alcopoppy spirits, regularly consumed by young women.

And single words, mostly from the Royal Liverpool University Hospital staff.

Artery. The study of paintings

Bacteria. Back door to cafe

Barium. What doctors do when patients die

Benign. What you be, after you be eight

Caesarean Section. A place in Rome

Catscan. Searching for kitty

Cauterize. Made eye contact with her

Colic. A sheepdog

Coma. A punctuation mark

Dilate. To live long

Enema. Not a friend

Fester. Quicker than someone else

Fibula. A small lie

Impotent. Distinguished, well known

Labour Pain. Getting hurt at work

Medical Staff. A doctor's cane

Morbid. A higher offer

Nitrates. Cheaper than day rates

Node. I knew it

Outpatient. A person who has fainted

Recovery Room. Place to do upholstery

Rectum. Nearly killed him

Secretion. Hiding something

Seizure. Roman emperor

Tablet. A small table

Terminal Illness. Getting sick at the airport

Tumour. One plus one more

Urine. Opposite of you're out

20

A WUNCH OF BANKERS

A new sign in the bank reads:

"Please note that this bank is installing new drive-through ATMs, enabling customers to withdraw cash without leaving their motors. Customers using this new facility are requested to use the procedures outlined below when accessing their accounts. After months of careful research, procedures have been developed. Please follow the appropriate steps for your geographical area."

Liverpool procedure:

1. Drive up to the cash machine.

2. Put down your car window.

3. Insert card into machine and enter PIN.

4. Enter amount of cash required and withdraw.

5. Retrieve card, cash and receipt.

6. Put window up.

7. Drive off.

Manchester procedure:

1. Drive up to cash machine.

2. Reverse and back up the required amount to align car window with the machine.

3. Pull on handbrake, put the window down.

4. Find wallet or handbag, tip all contents on to passenger seat to locate card.

5. Tell person on moby you will call them back and hang up.

6. Attempt to insert card into machine.

7. Open car door to allow easier access to machine due to its excessive distance from the car.

8. Insert card.

9. Reinsert card the right way round.

10. Dig through handbag or wallet once again to find diary with your PIN written on the inside back page.

11. Enter PIN.

12. Press cancel and re-enter correct PIN.

13. Enter amount of cash required.

14. Check queue of cars in rear view mirror. Sneer.

15. Retrieve cash and receipt.

16. Empty wallet or handbag again and place cash inside.

17. Instantly lose receipt.

18. Re-check queue of cars. Sneer.

19. Drive forward two feet.

20. Reverse back to cash machine.

21. Retrieve card.

22. Locate plastic card holder, and place card into the slot provided.

23. Give intimidating look to irate drivers waiting behind you.

24. Restart stalled engine and drive off.

25. Redial person on moby.

26. Drive for two or three miles.

27. Release handbrake.

21

IN THE PUB

A Cockney, a Scouser and a Manc were in a pub, talking about their sons.

"My son was born on St George's Day," commented the East Ender. "So we obviously decided to call him George."

"That's a real coincidence," remarked the Scouser. "My son was born on St Andrew's Day, so obviously we decided to call him Andrew."

"That's incredible, what a coincidence," said the Manc. "Exactly the same thing happened with my son, Pancake."

The Scouser stood at the bar for hours on end telling the bartender about his exploits.

"Now," said the bartender, "suppose you tell me something you can't do."

"Well," said the scally, "for one thing – I can't pay the bill."

A bloke walks into a Liverpool pub and asks for 12 pints of Guinness. A mere hour later, he's drunk them all. He then asks the barman:

"Do you sell shorts?"

"Yes" he replies.

"Have you got any in a 38 waist, then? I've just shit these."

In the same pub three guys are drinking in the bar when a drunk comes in, staggers up to them, and points at the guy in the middle, shouting, "Your mum's the best sex in Liverpool."

Everyone expects a fight, but the guy ignores him, so the drunk wanders off and bellies up to the bar at the far end.

Ten minutes later, the drunk comes back, points at the same guy, and says, "I just shagged your mum, and it was great."

Again the guy refuses to take the bait, and the drunk goes back to the far end of the bar.

Ten minutes later, he comes back and announces, "Your mum liked it!"

Finally the guy interrupts, "Go home, Dad, you're drunk!"

Scouser to mate in the pub: "I just read an article on the dangers of drinking. It scared the shit out of me. Bad breath, liver disease, brain shrinkage and lots of other stuff. So that's it. After today, no more reading."

22

IMPATIENT HOSPITALS

A guy is strolling past Ashworth Psychiatric Hospital in Maghull when he hears a loud chanting.

"Thirteen, thirteen, thirteen!" goes the noise from the hospital.

The man's curiosity gets the better of him, and he searches for a hole in the security fence. It's not long before he finds a small crack, so he leans forward and peers in.

Instantly, someone jabs him in the eye. As he reels back in agony, the chanting continues.

"Fourteen, fourteen, fourteen!"

A nurse walks into a room in Ashworth Psychiatric Hospital and sees a patient pretending he's driving a lorry, with his hands at 10 to 2.

The nurse asks him, "Kenny, what are you doing?"

Kenny replies, "Can't talk right now, I'm driving to Devon."

The nurse wishes him a good trip and leaves the room.

The next day the nurse enters Kenny's room just as he stops driving his imaginary truck and she asks, "Well Kenny, how was your trip?"

Kenny says, "I'm exhausted, I just got into Devon and I need some rest."

"That's great," replied the nurse, "I'm glad you had a safe trip."

The nurse leaves Kenny's room, and then goes across the hall into another patient's room and finds Davy sitting on his bed masturbating vigorously.

Shocked, she shouts, "Davy, what are you doing?"

To which Davy replies, "Shhh, I'm shagging Kenny's wife while he's in Devon."

23

LIFE AND DEATH

Scousers Mick and Paddy had promised their Uncle Seamus, who had been a seafaring gent all his life, to bury him at sea when he died. Of course, in due time, he did pass away and the boys kept their promise. They set off with Uncle Seamus all stitched up in a Liverpool flag bag and loaded him on to a hired rowing boat.

After a while Mick says, "Do you think this is far enough out, Paddy?"

Without a word Paddy slips over the side only to find himself standing in water up to his knees.

"This will never do, Mick. Let's row a bit more."

After a bit more rowing Paddy slips over the side again, but the water is only up to his belly, so they row on.

Again Mick asks Paddy, "Do you think this is far enough out Paddy?"

Once again Paddy slips over the side and almost immediately says, "No, this will never do." The water was only up to his chest.

So on they row and row and row and finally Paddy slips over the side and disappears. Quite a bit of time goes by and poor Mick is really getting himself into a state when suddenly Paddy breaks the surface gasping for breath.

"Well is it deep enough yet, Paddy?"

"Yer it is, hand me the shovel."

Three Scouse guys named Steve, Bruce and Kevin were working on a high-rise building. Steve falls off and is killed instantly.

As the ambulance takes the body away, Bruce says, "Despite the fact that she's a Manc, someone should go and tell his wife."

Kevin says, "OK, I'm pretty good at that sensitive stuff, I'll do it."

Two hours later, he comes back carrying a case of lager.

Bruce says, "Where did you get that, Kev?"

"Steve's wife gave it to me."

Bruce replies, "That's unbelievable, you told the woman her husband was dead and she gave you the beer?"

"Well, not exactly," Kevin said. "When she answered the door, I said to her: 'You must be Steve's widow.' She said, 'No, I'm not a widow.' And I said, 'I'll bet you a case of lager you are.'"